The Listening Earth

POEMS FROM THE COUNTRYSIDE
1400-2000

'In every clime, by every tongue,
Be God's surpassing glory sung;
Let all the listening earth be taught
The acts our great Redeemer wrought'

from Whitsuntide Hymn, 155

The Listening Earth

POEMS FROM THE COUNTRYSIDE
1400-2000

SELECTED BY JINNY BIRKBECK

First published by Merlin Unwin Books, Ludlow, in 2003.
This selection copyright © Jinny Birkbeck, 2003.

Merlin Unwin Books
Palmers House
7 Corve Street
Ludlow
Shropshire, UK
SY8 1DB
Email: books@merlinunwin.co.uk
Website: www.countrybooksdirect.com

ISBN 1 873674 60 0
Typeset by Merlin Unwin Books, Ludlow, UK.
Printed and bound in Great Britain by Biddles Ltd, Guildford.

All profits from the sales of this book will go into The Rank Foundation Fund, a charity that benefits country people whose livelihoods are threatened by the decline of farming and of rural businesses. The Rank Foundation Fund is administered by the ARC Addington Fund which itself was set up by the Archbishop of Canterbury as the Church of England's response to the hardship caused by the foot and mouth crisis in Britain in 2001.

For my father
HARRY BIRKBECK (1915 – 2003)
who first inspired me with a love of poetry
and of the Norfolk landscape where I grew up.

CONTENTS

[Note: titles in italics are those of works originally published separately.]

PART 1. THE WAY IT WAS

PART 2. A CELEBRATION

PART 3. DESTRUCTION

PART 4. SPIRIT OF PLACE

FOREWORD

I'm a townie. A willing townie, in London for most of my life, and then in Cheltenham for the last ten years. So when I see those opinion polls revealing the extraordinary percentages of people in towns and cities who aspire to live in the countryside, I must admit I find myself somewhat bemused! However, for the last thirty years or more, I've been a lover, a defender and an avid user of the countryside, in my work as an environmentalist and in my leisure time reconnecting with the natural world. When I can't be out there (which is a lot less often than I would like), then I can still read.

As I engage with today's poets, journalists and campaigners writing about the countryside, it's hard not to feel deep anxiety about the relationships we have with the land and the natural world in general. After fifty years of intensive farming here in the UK, with fewer and fewer people working on the land or even indirectly related to the land, the kind of intimate bonds that one finds celebrated in this anthology would appear to be weakening, becoming more attenuated, voyeuristic even. Yet many people continue to believe that without some vibrant connection back to the land, to nature's own rhythms and the cycles of food production, then the job of restoring a sustainable balance between our all too dominant species and the rest of life on Earth will remain all but impossible.

Poetry has an important part to play in re-establishing those connections, in reminding us of what it means to be in 'a state of grace' in the face of Nature. I have no doubt that this anthology will play an important part in that reconnection process.

Jonathon Porritt
4 July 2002

INTRODUCTION

There was a post-war sense of loss and desolation as I was growing up in the forties. Yet as children we didn't like innovations; they were threatening. When I was ten the first sign-post came to the Norfolk village where I grew up. Three of us struggled with this crude intrusion into our quiet world until we had finally managed to push it over, flat to the ground. Then came the pylons. At fourteen I was prepared to go to prison rather than let anyone fell our trees to fit the pylons in. Now it is hard to find a lowland landscape without them. Attitudes towards landscape and lifestyles have changed inexorably, although W. G. Hoskins said the Old English 'had not eye for scenery any more than other hard-working farmers of later centuries…they were too busy fighting against roots and bramble'. Now many have no eye for scenery, so intent are they on driving through traffic to their supermarket.

As a child I rode a pony across the great Norfolk fields whose contours encompassed my world. The height and depth of my universe was there. My first fear was of the cold in the woods when out beating for the pheasant shoots. Many of the beaters were the wives of the farm men and keepers who loved a day out away from their kitchens and gardens, out in the open, jumping and sometimes falling into the great ditches, laughing and gossiping with their friends as they earned a day's wage. I felt awe and reverence for time 'long ago' as I stood for the first time at the smooth edges of a pingo (a pool formed during the Ice Age) on the Common, a wild tract of land where the horsetail and meadow sweet grow amongst reeds and bulrushes, and strange mis-shapen thorn bushes confuse the eye in all directions. The loudest noise we knew was the sound of thunder. Elvis Presley and others had their place as I grew up, but only within the house. The idea of carrying a radio to a beauty spot would have seemed shocking and wicked. I heard tell of a school outing on the Yorkshire moors; the whole class, moved by a sudden youthful pantheistic reverence for the Nature they had just seen, began singing hymns on the coach. (They were severely reprimanded for irreverence.)

And finally there was my father to whom this book is dedicated. A greater countryman never lived. He knew and cherished his environment. He farmed with love for his acres and for the people living thereon. He fished on the little chalk stream that ran through our farm with a dry fly on summer evenings, he beagled in the afternoons teaching us children to jump the ditches and to understand the chase. He coursed with our greyhounds and with the lurchers that ran at our heels when we rode; but no-one was allowed to shoot a hare for fun. They were beautiful and special we were told. Only at the very end of the season was a careful cull by the keepers allowed, to keep the hare population healthy and controlled. He hunted the fox and shot partridge, pheasant and what was known as 'various' at the end of a day's sport. And then at bedtime he would read for us the poetry of the chase; of the English countryside and of the Australian outback. He kept a drawer full of the wonderful poems he had come across.

My father's attitude to the children growing up around him could be summed up in his letter to me on facing my school certificate exams: 'Don't worry about these exams, they're not important. What *is* important is to watch out for Whitethroats sitting on telegraph wires.' These summer visitors generally arrived mid-April, but their Autumn migration to the Continent began late July (School exam time). He taught us to look and learn about the trees, birds, butterflies and animals; their habits and their habitats. As a farmer he showed us how to tell the quality of the crops, how to judge when a field is ready for cutting. In harvest-time we travelled on the corn-trailers back and forth from cornfield to dresser until night fell and the sparks flying upwards from those vertical tractor exhaust pipes mingled with the stars above.

My first job was pulling ragwort at sixpence an acre; my second, pulling wild oats out of the corn at fifteen shillings a day. I remember sleeping in the corner of a field at lunchtime, those bundles of wild oats were so heavy. But like many a country child, I was destined to spend most of my adult life working in the city. In my early twenties I was employed by The Council For The Protection of Rural England. I was unhappy living in a city but knew that for the time being I could not return to my childhood environment. I was in exile, and over the next thirty years I tempered malaise by reading poetry, and found refuge by escaping into the country whenever possible.

In the sixties our country ways and pursuits did not seem under threat as they do now. The demands of modern urban life, the steady encroachment of modern lifestyles with their need for constant speed and instant satisfaction hadn't gathered momentum. We still exclaimed in outrage when familiar beauty spots began to show off their 'facilities', and petrol stations, once so discreetly camouflaged, became bright with garish colours. Trees once given the respect due to their age, began to be felled at the planners' whim. These things are now accepted as inevitable. An exciting new word 'Progress' began to be bandied about. It was changing the landscape of my youth and sweeping away the tranquillity, the sense of continuity and the certainties that had gone with it. Poetry, I told myself, could do battle with this demon.

At the beginning of the industrial revolution, it was thought right and proper to admire the new urbanisation, the great mills and factories, and much prosperity was born from them. But this anthology was conceived as a means of supporting not those who submerge 'grass under concrete', nor those who, though spending their weekends in the country, depend on sources elsewhere for their income. It is for those people who live and work in the countryside, interdependent on one another.

We recognise the healing respite that the countryside holds and that country people symbolise. Our countryside cannot be seen merely as an agricultural wealth machine: and wildlife must be more than something that exists in exotic places seen on television.

Many of us associate childhood with memories of a country world both precious and vanishing; almost a lost world. Most of us still dream of an impossible reunion with childhood itself. Poetry can temper our understanding of reality and sustain our vision for the future.

Jinny Birkbeck
January 2003

PART ONE

THE WAY IT WAS

Virgil (70-19 BC)

Publius Vergilius Maro. Great Roman poet of the Aeneid, the Eclogues and the Georgics. Pervasive influence throughout the centuries. Wrote poems in the Greek pastoral tradition, which idealised country life, but added new depth by alluding to topics of contemporary interest.

from ECLOGUE I

[MELIBŒUS TO TITYRUS]
But we depart, to thirsty Africa
Chalk-rolling Oxus[1], and the Scythian wolds[2]
Or Britons wholly sundered from the world.
Ah! shall I ever long years hence behold
My own dear home—a wretched bothy then
With turf-piled roof—and marvel as I gaze
At a few ears of corn, my realm of old?

1. Now called the Amu-Darya River flowing between Uzbekistan and Turkmenistan into the Aral sea.
2. Ancient country North East of the Black Sea.

William Blake (1757-1827)

Visionary, painter, engraver and poet. Son of a hosier, Blake never went to school. Apprenticed to an engraver; later became a student at the Royal Academy. Married the daughter of a market gardener. Lifetime of engraving, writing, publishing. Died poor, considered gifted but eccentric by fellow writers.

THE NEW JERUSALEM

And did those feet in ancient time
Walk upon England's mountains green?
And was the holy Lamb of God
On England's pleasant pastures seen?

And did the Countenance Divine
Shine forth upon our clouded hills?
And was Jerusalem builded here
Among these dark Satanic Mills?

Bring me my Bow of burning gold!
Bring me my Arrows of desire!
Bring me my Spear: O clouds, unfold!
Bring me my Chariot of fire!

I will not cease from Mental Fight,
Nor shall my Sword sleep in my hand,
Till we have built Jerusalem
In England's green and pleasant Land.

Geoffrey Chaucer (c.1343-1400)

Son of a London vintner. Fought with Edward III's invading army in France. Married into patron John of Gaunt's family. Held diplomatic and court posts including customs controller at a London port. French and Italian influences. Lived in Kent from 1386 till death.

from THE WIFE OF BATH'S TALE

Now in the olden days of King Arthur,
Of whom the Britons speak with great honour,
All this wide land was land of faëry.
The elf-queen, with her jolly company,
Danced oftentimes on many a green mead;
This was the old opinion, as I read.
I speak of many hundred years ago;
But now no man can see the elves, you know.
For now the so-great charity and prayers
Of limiters[1] and other holy friars
That do infest each land and every stream
As thick as motes are in a bright sunbeam,
Blessing halls, chambers, kitchens, ladies' bowers
Cities and towns and castles and high towers,
Manors and barns and stables, aye and dairies—
This causes it that there are now no fairies.
For where was wont to walk full many an elf,
Right there walks now the limiter himself
In noons and afternoons and in mornings,
Saying his matins and such holy things,
As he goes round his district in his gown.
Women may now go safely up and down,
In every copse or under every tree;
There is no other incubus[2] than he,
And would do them nothing but dishonour.

1. Friars who had a licence to beg within certain bounds.
2. Nightmare or devil in a male body.

Sir Philip Sidney (1554-1586)

Educated at Shewsbury School and Oxford. Travelled the continent. Painted by Veronese. Knighted by Elizabeth I. Man of letters. Great Renaissance figure. Patron of the arts, a soldier, lover and courtier.

from COUNTESS OF PEMBROKE'S ARCADIA

O sweet woods the delight of solitarines!
O how much I do like your solitarines!
Where man's mind hath a freed consideration
Of goodnes to receive lovely direction.
Where senses do behold th'order of heav'nly hoste,
And wise thoughts do behold what the creator is:
Contemplation here holdeth his only seate:
Bownded with no limitts, borne with a wing of a hope
Clymes even under the starres, Nature is under it.

Nought disturbs thy quiet, all to thy service yeeld,
Each sight draws on a thought, thought mother of science,
Sweet birds kindly do graunt harmony unto thee,
Faire trees' shade is enough fortification,
Nor danger to thy selfe if be not in thy selfe.

O sweete woods the delight of solitarines!
O how much I do like your solitarines!
Here no treason is hidd, vailed in innocence,
Nor envie's snaky ey, finds any harbor here,
Nor flatterers' venomous insinuations,
Nor conning humorists' puddled opinions,
Nor courteous ruin of proffered usury,
Nor time pratled away, cradle of ignorance,
Nor causelesse duty, nor comber[1] of arrogance,
Nor trifling title of vanity dazleth us,
Nor golden manacles, stand for a paradise,
Here wrong's name is unheard: slander a monster is.

6

Keepe thy sprite from abuse, here no abuse doth haunte.
What man grafts in a tree dissimulation?

O sweete woods the delight of solitarines!
O how well I do like your solitarines!
Yet deare soile, if a soule closed in a mansion
As sweete as violetts, faire as a lilly is,
Streight as Cedar, a voice staines[2] the Cannary birds,
Whose shade safety doth hold, danger avoideth her:
Such wisedome, that in her lives speculation:
Such goodnes that in her simplicitie triumphs:
Where envie's snaky ey, winketh or els dyeth,
Slander wants a pretext, flattery gone beyond:
Oh! if such a one have bent to a lonely life
Her stepps, gladd we receave, gladd we receave her eys.
And thinke not she doth hurt our solitarines,
 For such company decks such solitarines.

1. Long foaming wave.
2. Shames.

Andrew Marvell (1621-1678)

Son of a Yorkshire parson. Moved to Hull, then studied at Cambridge. Travelled on continent during Civil War learning languages; later travelled as a diplomatic secretary. Famed in his day as patriot, satirist, and foe to tyranny. Now esteemed as a lyric poet.

THE MOWER TO THE GLOW-WORMS

I

Ye living lamps by whose dear light
The nightingale does sit so late
And studying all the summer-night,
Her matchless songs does meditate;

II

Ye country comets that portend
No war nor prince's funeral,
Shining unto no higher end
Than to presage the grass's fall;

III

Ye glow-worms, whose officious flame
To wandering mowers shows the way,
That in the night have lost their aim,
And after foolish fires do stray;

IV

Your courteous lights in vain you waste,
Since Juliana here is come,
For she my mind hath so displaced,
That I shall never find my home.

George Crabbe (1754-1832)

Born in Aldeburgh, Suffolk. Father was a collector of salt-duties. Became parish doctor before becoming writer and curate. Studied botany. *The Village* established his reputation as a poet who rejected the conventions of the pastoral tradition, painting instead a detailed picture of rural poverty and a blighted landscape.

from THE VILLAGE

I grant indeed that fields and flocks have charms
For him that grazes or for him that farms;
But when amid such pleasing scenes I trace
The poor laborious natives of the place,
And see the mid-day sun, with fervid ray,
On their bare heads and dewy temples play;
While some, with feebler heads and fainter hearts,
Deplore their fortune, yet sustain their parts—
Then shall I dare these real ills to hide
In tinsel trappings of poetic pride?
No; cast by Fortune on a frowning coast,
Which neither groves nor happy valleys boast;
Where other cares than those the Muse relates,
And other shepherds dwell with other mates;
By such examples taught, I paint the cot,
As Truth will paint it, and as bards will not:
Nor you, ye poor, of lettered scorn complain,
To you the smoothest song is smooth in vain;
O'ercome by labor, and bowed down by time,
Feel you the barren flattery of a rhyme?
Can poets soothe you, when you pine for bread,
By winding myrtles round your ruined shed?
Can their light tales your weighty griefs o'erpower,
Or glad with airy mirth the toilsome hour?

John Keats (1795-1821)

Son of manager of livery stables at Moorfields, Keats was orphaned at 14; a year later he was apprenticed to an apothecary-surgeon. In spite of precarious finances, he abandoned his profession for poetry at 21. Became engaged to his great love Fanny Brawne. Invited by Shelley to Italy where he died in Rome. Tennyson considered him to be the greatest poet of the 19th Century.

MEG MERRILIES

Old Meg she was a gipsy,
And lived upon the moors,
Her bed it was the brown heath turf,
And her house was out of doors.

Her apples were swart blackberries,
Her currents pods o' broom
Her wine was dew o' the wild white rose,
Her book a churchyard tomb.

Her brothers were the craggy hills,
Her sisters larchen trees –
Alone with her great family
She lived as she did please.

No breakfast had she many a morn,
No dinner many a noon,
And 'stead of supper she would stare
Full hard against the moon.

But every morn of woodbine fresh
She made her garlanding,
And every night the dark glen yew
She wove, and she would sing.

And with her fingers old and brown
She plaited mats o' rushes,
And gave them to the cottagers
She met among the bushes.

Old Meg was brave as Margaret Queen
And tall as Amazon,
An old red blanket cloak she wore,
A chip-hat had she on.
God rest her aged bones somewhere –
She died full long agone.

Robert Burns (1759-1796)

One of seven children born to Ayrshire cotter. He began writing poetry at school while employed in spare time as ploughman and labourer on the family farm. Poverty and injustice led him to support the French Revolution. Public success followed publication of *Poems Chiefly in the Scottish Dialect* in 1786. Attractive and gregarious, he married in 1788 after a series of entanglements with women.

TO A MOUSE/ TAY A MOOS

On turning her up in her Nest, with the Plough, November, 1785.
(As originally printed in the Kilmarnock edition.)

Old English

> Wee, sleeket, cowran, tim'rous beastie,
> 0, what a panic's in thy breastie!
> Thou need na start awa sae hasty,
>   Wi' bickering brattle!
> I wad be laith to rin an' chase thee,
>   Wi' murd'ring *pattle*!
> I'm truly sorry Man's dominion
> Has broken Nature's social union,
> An' justifies that ill opinion,
>   Which makes thee startle,
> At me, thy poor, earth-born companion,
>   An' *fellow-mortal*!
>
> I doubt na, whyles, but thou may *thieve*;
> What then ? poor beastie, thou maun live!
> A *daimen-icker* in a *thrave*
>   'S a sma' request
> I'll get a blessin wi' the lave,
>   An' never miss 't
> Thy wee-bit *housie*, too, in ruin!
> It's silly wa's the win's are strewin !

An' naething, now, to big a new ane,
      O' foggage green !
An' bleak *December's winds* ensuin.
      Baith snell an' keen!

Thou saw the fields laid bare an wast,
An' weary *Winter* comin fast,
An' cozie here, beneath the blast,
      Thou thought to dwell,
Till crash ! the cruel *coulter* past
      Out thro' thy cell.

That wee-bit heap o' leaves an' stibble,
Has cost thee monie a weary nibble!
Now thou's turn'd out, for a' thy trouble,
      But house or hald,
To thole the Winter's *sleety dribble*,
      An' cranreuch cauld!

But Mousie, thou are no thy-lane,
In proving *foresight* may be vain:
The best laid schemes o' *Mice* an' *Men*,
      Gang aft agley,
An' lea'e us nought but grief an' pain,
      For promis'd joy!

Still, thou art blest, compar'd wi' *me*!
The *present* only toucheth thee:
But Och ! I *backward* cast my e'e,
      On prospects drear!
An' *forward*, tho' I canna see,
      I *guess* an' *fear*!

To a Mouse / Tay a Moos

In Ayrshire Scotch

Wee, sleekit, coorun, timrus beestie,
Oa hwit a panic's in thii breestie
Thoo neednay stert uwaw say haistie,
   Wi bickurin brattul!
A wud bee laith tay yin un chais thee,
   Wi murdrin pattul!

A'm troolie soaray Man'z doameenyun
Hiz broakun Naitur'z soashul yoonyun,
Un justifeez that ull oapednyun,
   Thut maks thee stertul
At mee, thii pair, yirth-boarn coampanyun,
   Un falla-moartul!

A dootnay, hweilz, bitt thoo may theev;
Hwit than ? pair beestie, thoo mun leev!
A daimun ickur in a threev
   'Z a smaw riquest:
A'll get a blessin wi the laiv,
   Un nivvur miss't.
Thii wee bit hoosie, tay, in rooin!
Its sullie wawz the wunz ar strooin!
Un naything noo,—tay big a nyoo yin—
   Oa fuggij green!
Un bleek Dizembur'z wunz insooin,
   Baith snell un keen

Thou saw the feelz laid hair un waist,
Un weerie wuntur cummin fast,
Un coazie heer uneeth the blast,
   Thoo thoakht tay dwell (dwall),
Tull crash! the crooul cootur past
   Oot throo thii sell.

That wee bit heep oa leefs un stibbul!
Hiz coast thee munnie a weerie nibbul!
Noo thoo'z turnt oot, fur aw thii tribbul,
        But hoos or hawl,
Tay thoal the wuntur'z sleetie dribbul,
        Un crawnrukh cawl.

But, Moosie, thou ert noa thii lain,
In praivin foarsikht may bee vain:
The best-laid scaimz oa meis un men
        Gang aft uglei,
Un lee us noakht but greef un pain
        Fur proamist joaie.

Still, thoo ert blest, cumpaird wi mee
The praizunt oanlie tuchiz thee:
But Oakh! A backwurd cast ma ee
        Oan proaspiks dreer!
Un furrit, thoa A cannay see,
        A gais un feer!

In modern English

Little, sleek, cowering, timorous creature!
Oh, what a panic's in thy little breast!
Thou need'st not start away so hastily,
With hurried rush
I should, be loath to run and chase thee,
With murdering plough-staff
I'm truly sorry Man's dominion
Has broken Nature's social union,
And justifies that ill opinion,
Which makes thee start
At me, thy poor, earth-born companion,
And fellow-mortal!
I doubt not that thou may'st steal sometimes.
What then, poor little thing, thou must live

15

An occasional ear of corn in twenty-four sheaves
            Is a small request:
I'll get a blessing with the rest,
            And never miss it
Thy tiny house, too, in ruin!
The winds are strewing its weak walls.
And nothing now—to build a new one—
            Of green herbage!
And bleak December's winds approaching,
            Both sharp and keen!

Thou saw'st the fields laid bare and waste,
And weary Winter coming fast,
And cosily here, below the blast.
            Thou thought'st to dwell,
Till crash! the cruel coulter passed
            Right through thy cell.

That little heap of leaves and stubble
Has cost thee many a weary nibble!
Now thou'rt turned out, notwithstanding all thy trouble,
            Without house or home (hold),
To endure the winter's sleety drizzle,
            And hoarfrost cold.
But, little mouse, thou art not alone
In proving foresight may be vain
The best-laid schemes of mice and men
            Go often awry,
And leave it's nought but grief and pain,
            Instead of promised joy!
Still, thou art blest, compared with me!
The present only toucheth thee:
But O! I backward cast my eye
            On prospects drear!
And forward, though I cannot see,

            I guess and fear!

THE PLOUGHMAN

The ploughman he's a bonnie lad.
His mind is ever true, jo.
His garters knit below his knee.
His bonnet it is blue, jo.

Then up wi't a', my ploughman lad.
And hey, my merry ploughman;
Of a' the trades that I do ken.
Commend me to the ploughman.

My ploughman he comes hame at e' en.
He's aften wat and weary;
Cast off the wat, put on the dry.
And gae to bed, my Dearie!

I will wash my ploughman's hose.
And I will dress his o'erlay;
I will mak my ploughman s bed.
And cheer him late and early.

I hae been east. I hae been west.
I hae been at Saint Johnston[1] ;
The bonniest sight that e'er I saw
Was the ploughman laddie dancin'.

Snaw-white stockin's on his legs.
And siller buckles glancin';
A gude blue bonnet on his head.
And O. but he was handsome!

Commend me to the barn-yard.
And the corn-mow, man;
I never gat my coggie fou[2]
Till I met wi' the ploughman.

1. Saint Johnston is in Perth.
2. 'coggie fou' means full pail.

John Clare (1793-1864)

Son of a farm labourer in Northamptonshire. Became hedge setter and
day labourer. The parting from his first love, Mary Joyce and moving
four miles from his birthplace disturbed him deeply. Certified as
insane, he spent the last twenty-seven years of his life in asylums,
where he continued to write poetry.

STRAY WALKS

How pleasant are the fields to roam & think
Whole sabbaths through unnoticed & alone
Beside the little molehill skirted brink
Of the small brook that skips oer many a stone
Of green woodside where many a squatting oak
Far oer grass screeds their white stained branches hing
Forming in pleasant close a happy seat
To nestle in while small birds chirp & sing
& the loud blackbird will its mate provoke
More louder yet its chorus to repeat
How pleasant is it thus to think & roam
The many paths scarce knowing which to chuse
All full of pleasant scenes — then wander home
& oer the beautys we have met to muse

Alfred Edward Housman (1859-1936)

Studied at Oxford where his passionate attachment to Moses Jackson provided the inspiration for later verse. Worked as a clerk at the Patent Office in London while publishing scholarly work on Roman poets. Became Professor of Latin at University College, London and later at Cambridge. Published *A Shropshire Lad* at his own expense.

'ON MOONLIT HEATH AND LONESOME BANK'
(*from A SHROPSHIRE LAD*)

On moonlit heath and lonesome bank
The sheep beside me graze;
And yon the gallows used to clank
Fast by the four cross ways.

A careless shepherd once would keep
The flocks by moonlight there,
And high amongst the glimmering sheep
The dead man stood on air.

They hang us now in Shrewsbury jail:
The whistles blow forlorn,
And trains all night groan on the rail
To men that die at morn.

There sleeps in Shrewsbury jail tonight,
Or wakes, as may betide,
A better lad, if things went right,
Than most that sleep outside.

And naked to the hangman's noose
The morning clocks will ring
A neck God made for other use
Than strangling in a string.

And sharp the link of life will snap,
And dead on air will stand
Heels that held up as straight a chap
As treads upon the land.

So here I'll watch the night and wait
To see the morning shine,
When he will hear the stroke of eight
And not the stroke of nine;

And wish my friend as sound a sleep
As lads I did not know,
That shepherded the moonlit sheep
A hundred years ago.

Thomas Hardy (1840-1928)

Born in Dorchester, Dorset. Son of a stonemason. Worked for an architect in London. Considered taking holy orders but lost his faith.
Returned to Dorchester in 1867, continued work as an architect and
began writing first novel (unpublished). The success in 1874 of *Far
from the Madding Crowd* enabled him to give up architecture for
writing. Public honours and royal recognition culminated in
Westminster Abbey funeral.

WE FIELD-WOMEN

>   How it rained
> When we worked at Flintcomb-Ash,
> And could not stand upon the hill
> Trimming swedes for the slicing-mill.
> The wet washed through us – plash, plash, plash:
>   How it rained!
>
>   How it snowed
> When we crossed from Flintcomb-Ash
> To the Great Barn for drawing reed,
> Since we could nowise chop a swede. –
> Flakes in each doorway and casement-sash:
>   How it snowed!
>
>   How it shone
> When we went from Flintcomb Ash
> To start at dairywork once more
> In the laughing meads, with cows three-score,
> And pails, and songs, and love – too rash:
>   How it shone!

THE MILKMAID

Under a daisied bank
There stands a rich red ruminating cow,
And hard against her flank
A cotton-hooded milkmaid bends her brow.

The flowery river-ooze
Upheaves and falls; the milk purrs in the pail;
Few pilgrims but would choose
The peace of such a life in such a vale.

The maid breathes words — to vent,
It seems, her sense of Nature's scenery,
Of whose life, sentiment,
And essence, very part itself is she.

She bends a glance of pain.
And, at a moment, lets escape a tear;
Is it that passing train,
Whose alien whirr offends her country ear? –

Nay! Phyllis does not dwell
On visual and familiar things like these;
What moves her is the spell
Of inner themes and inner poetries:

Could but by Sunday morn
Her gay new gown come, meads might dry to dun,
Trains shriek till ears were torn,
If Fred would not prefer that Other One.

Robert Graves (1895-1985)

Born in London, the son of Alfred Perceval Graves. Joined the Royal Welsh Fusiliers aged 19 and served in the trenches for two years of World War I. Returned severely injured and suffering from shell-shock. Married first wife, Laura, 1918. Studied at Oxford, 1919. Wrote powerful autobiography, *Goodbye to All That,* in 1929. Lived in Majorca with second wife, Beryl, from 1946 till death. A prolific poet and novelist.

LOVE WITHOUT HOPE[1]

Love without hope, as when the young bird-catcher
Swept off his tall hat to the Squire's own daughter,
So let the imprisoned larks escape and fly
Singing about her head, as she rode by.

---

1. Paints the picture of a poor country lad so overcome by the beauty of the squire's daughter that he doffs his hat to her and in doing so casts away carelessly his only means of survival (selling larks at the local market).

Wilfred Scawen Blunt (1840-1922)

Poet, diplomat, traveller, anti-imperialist and Arabist. Married Byron's granddaughter. Worked in support of Egyptian, Indian and Irish independence. Had a brief spell in an Irish Prison.

THE OLD SQUIRE

I like the hunting of the hare
  Better than that of the fox;
I like the joyous morning air,
  And the crowing of the cocks.

I like the calm of the early fields,
  The ducks asleep by the lake,
The quiet hour which Nature yields,
  Before mankind is awake.

I like the pheasants and feeding things
  Of the unsuspicious morn;
I like the flap of the wood-pigeon's wings
  As she rises from the corn.

I like the blackbird's shriek, and his rush
  From the turnips as I pass by,
And the partridge hiding her head in a bush,
  For her young ones cannot fly.

I like these things, and I like to ride,
  When all the world is in bed,
To the top of the hill where the sky grows wide,
  And where the sun grows red.

The beagles at my horse heels trot,
  In silence after me;
There's Ruby, Roger, Diamond, Dot,
  Old Slut and Margery,

24

A score of names well used, and dear,
  The names my childhood knew;
The horn, with which I rouse their cheer,
  Is the horn my father blew.

I like the hunting of the hare
  Better than that of the fox;
The new world still is all less fair
  Than the old world it mocks.

I covet not a wider range
  Than these dear manors give;
I take my pleasures without change
  And as I lived I live.

I leave my neighbours to their thought;
  My choice it is, and pride,
On my own lands to find my sport.,
  In my own fields to ride.

The hare herself no better loves
  The field where she was bred,
Than I the habit of these groves,
  My own inherited.

I know my quarries every one
  The meuse where she sits low;
The road she chose to-day was run
  A hundred years ago.

The lags, the gills, the forest ways,
  The hedgerows one and all,
These are the kingdoms of my chase,
  And bounded by my wall;

Nor has the world a better thing,
  Though one should search it round,
Than thus to live one's own sole king,
  Upon one's own sole ground.

I like the hunting of the hare;
  It brings me, day by day,
The memory of old days as fair,
  With dead men past away.

To these, as homeward still I ply
  And past the churchyard gate,
Where all are laid as I must lie,
  I stop and raise my hat.

I like the hunting of the hare;
  New sports I hold in scorn.
I like to be as my fathers were,
  In the days ere I was born.

Gilbert Keith Chesterton (1874-1936)

A literary critic, essayist, novelist and writer of short stories – famously 'Father Brown', a crime-solving East Anglian priest. Made his name in journalism during the Boer War; he was anti-imperial, pro-Boer. A friend of Hilaire Belloc. Became a Roman Catholic in 1922. His writings celebrated the diversity of people and places.

THE ROLLING ENGLISH ROAD

Before the Roman came to Rye or out to Severn strode,
The rolling English drunkard made the rolling English road.
A reeling road, a rolling road, that rambles round the shire,
And after him the parson ran, the sexton and the squire;
A merry road, a mazy road, and such as we did tread
The night we went to Birmingham by way of Beachy Head.

I knew no harm of Bonaparte and plenty of the Squire.
And for to fight the Frenchman I did not much desire;
But I did bash their baggonets because they came arrayed
To straighten out the crooked road an English drunkard made,
Where you and I went down the lane with ale-mugs in our hands,
The night we went to Glastonbury by way of Goodwin Sands.

His sins they were forgiven him; or why do flowers run
Behind him; and the hedges all strengthening in the sun?
The wild thing went from left to right and knew not which was which,
But the wild rose was above him when they found him in the ditch.
God pardon us, nor harden us; we did not see so clear
The night we went to Bannockburn by way of Brighton Pier.

My friends, we will not go again or ape an ancient rage,
Or stretch the folly of our youth to be the shame of age,
But walk with clearer eyes and ears this path that wandereth,
And see undrugged in evening light the decent inn of death;
For there is good news yet to hear and fine things to be seen,
Before we go to Paradise by way of Kensal Green.

27

Edward Thomas (1878-1917)

Educated at Oxford. Married young and left London for Kent where he supported the family by writing biographies, topographies and reviews. Produced more than forty books. Began writing poetry in 1913; in 1915 he enlisted in the army and was killed at Arras.

ADLESTROP

Yes. I remember Adlestrop—
The name, because one afternoon
Of heat the express-train drew up there
Unwontedly. It was late June.

The steam hissed. Someone cleared his throat.
No one left and no one came
On the bare platform. What I saw
Was Adlestrop—only the name.

And willows, willow-herb, and grass,
And meadowsweet, and haycocks dry,
No whit less still and lonely fair
Than the high cloudlets in the sky.

And for that minute a blackbird sang
Close by, and round him, mistier,
Farther and farther, all the birds
Of Oxfordshire and Gloucestershire.

Robert Frost (1874-1936)

American poet, born and raised in San Francisco. Moved to New England where he learnt to make shoes, edited a country paper, taught and farmed. Lived 1912-15 in England with his family and published his first poetry. Hailed as the American heir to Wordsworth and Emerson in his response to nature.

MOWING

There was never a sound beside the wood but one,
And that was my long scythe whispering to the ground.
What was it it whispered? I knew not well myself;
Perhaps it was something about the heat of the sun,
Something, perhaps, about the lack of sound—
And that was why it whispered and did not speak.
It was no dream of the gift of idle hours,
Or easy gold at the hand of fay or elf:
Anything more than the truth would have seemed too weak
To the earnest love that laid the swale in rows,
Not without feeble-pointed spikes of flowers
(Pale orchises), and scared a bright green snake.
The fact is the sweetest dream that labour knows.
My long scythe whispered and left the hay to make.

Edmund Blunden (1896-1974)

Born in London, childhood spent in Kent. Educated at Christ's Hospital and Oxford. Survived the war fighting in the trenches, later wrote war poems. His best-known work *Undertones of War* (published in 1928) describes the double destruction of man and nature in Flanders. The Kent countryside features prominently in his poetry.

FOREFATHERS

Here they went with smock and crook,
  Toiled in the sun, lolled in the shade,
Here they mudded out the brook
  And here their hatchet cleared the glade:
Harvest-supper woke their wit,
Huntsman's moon their wooings lit.

From this church they led their brides,
  From this church themselves were led
Shoulder-high; on these waysides
  Sat to take their beer and bread.
Names are gone—what men they were
These their cottages declare.

Names are vanished, save the few
  In the old brown Bible scrawled;
These were men of pith and thew,
  Whom the city never called;
Scarce could read or hold a quill,
Built the barn, the forge, the mill.

On the green they watched their sons
  Playing till too dark to see,
As their fathers watched them once
  As my father once watched me
While the bat and beetle flew
On the warm air webbed with dew.

Unrecorded, unrenowned,
  Men from whom my ways begin,
Here I know you by your ground
  But I know you not within—
There is silence, there survives
Not a moment of your lives.

Like the bee that now is blown
  Honey-heavy on my hand,
From his toppling tansy-throne
  In the green tempestuous land—
I'm in clover now, nor know
Who made honey long ago.

Andrew Young (1885-1971)

Born in Scotland. Educated in Edinburgh. Ordained minister first to the Free Church in 1912, then to the Church of England in 1939. Had a lifelong interest in botany and the natural world.

THE SHEPHERD'S HUT

The smear of blue peat smoke
That staggered on the wind and broke,
The only sign of life,
Where was the shepherd's wife,
Who left those flapping clothes to dry,
Taking no thought for her family?
For, as they bellied out
And limbs took shape and waved about,
I thought, She little knows
That ghosts are trying on her children's clothes

Austin Clarke (1896-1974)

Irish poet, playwright and novelist. Born in Dublin, educated at Belvedere College and University College Dublin. After fifteen years as a journalist in England, he returned to Ireland to publish eighteen volumes of poetry. Had a great interest in reviving verse drama.

THE FAIR AT WINDGAP

There was airy music and sport at the fair
And showers were tenting on the bare field,
Laughter had knotted a crowd where the horses
And mares were backing, when carts from the wheel-wright
Were shafted: bargains on sale everywhere and the barmen
Glassing neat whiskey or pulling black porter
On draught—and O the red brandy, the oatmeal
And the whiteness of flour in the weighing scale!

Callico petticoats, cashmere and blouses,
Blankets of buttermilk, flannel on stalls there,
Caps of bright tweed and corduroy trousers
And green or yellow ribbon with a stripe;
The tanner was hiding, the saddler plied the bradawl;[1]
Barrows had chinaware, knives and blue razors,
Black twisted tobacco to pare in the claypipe
And the ha'penny harp that is played on a finger.

Soft as rain slipping through rushes, the cattle
Came: dealers were brawling at seven-pound-ten,
On heifers in calf a bargain was clapped
When ewes, that are nearer the grass, had taken
Two guineas; the blacksmith was filing the horn in his lap
For the fillies called up more hands than their height,
Black goats were cheap; for a sow in the stock
O Flaherty got but the half of her farrow.

Balladmen, beggarmen, trick o' the loop men
And cardmen, hiding Queen Maeve up their sleeve,
Were picking red pennies and soon a prizefighter
Enticed the young fellows and left them all grieving:
While the marriageable girls were walking up and down
And the folk were saying that the Frenchmen
Had taken the herring from the brown tide
And sailed at daybreak, they were saying.

Twenty-five tinkers that came from Glentartan,
Not counting the jennets[2] and barefooted women,
Had a white crop of metal upon every cart;
The neighbours were buying, but a red-headed man
Of them, swearing no stranger could bottom a kettle,
Leaped over the droves going down to the ocean,
Glibbed with the sunlight: blows were around him
And so the commotion arose at the fair.

1. Small boring tool.
2. Small Spanish horse.

Ronald Stuart Thomas (1913-2000)

Born in Cardiff. A poet and a clergyman. His poetry derives from working in remote rural communities in a bleak landscape. Many unite religious and rural imagery.

ON THE FARM

There was Dai Puw. He was no good.
They put him in the fields to dock swedes,
And took the knife from him, when he came home
At late evening with a grin
Like the slash of a knife on his face.

There was Llew Puw, and he was no good.
Every evening after the ploughing
With the big tractor he would sit in his chair,
And stare into the tangled fire garden,
Opening his slow lips like a snail.

There was Huw Puw, too. What shall I say?
I have heard him whistling in the hedges
On and on, as though winter
Would never again leave those fields,
And all the trees were deformed.

And lastly there was the girl:
Beauty under some spell of the beast.
Her pale face was the lantern
By which they read in life's dark book
The shrill sentence: God is love.

Michael Hamburger (b.1924)

Born of a German family which emigrated to Scotland and then England in 1933. A translator and critic as well as a poet.

from BERKSHIRE'S ANCIENT MAN

He can't be walking there now,
His head, bird-like, stuck out,
Ever so slightly tilted
Not for looking askance
At the new housing estate,
Not for looking at all
At the changes, mattresses dumped
In the ditches along the lane,
Nor stopping, except to roll
A fag or, for less than a minute,
Chat with us, chuckle
Over the rare good luck
Of having survived so long,
Outlived his wife, his acquaintance
And his very calling of coachman.
Cars didn't bother him.
No, horses it was
Had done for his father, his brother,
His father's father before them,
All coachmen or grooms in their time.

Suppose that his luck held,
The lane is a lane still,
No car knocked him down:
Near-centenarian then,
A decade ago and more,
He can't be walking there now.

George Mackay Brown (1921-96)

Scottish poet and novelist, born on the Orkneys where he spent most of his life. Poems inspired by Norse saga, island folklore and the cycle of country life.

ROADS

The road to the burn
Is pails, gossip, gray linen.

The road to the shore
Is salt and tar.

We call the track to the peats
The kestrel road.

The road to the kirk
Is a road of silences.

Ploughmen's feet
Have beaten a road to the lamp and barrel.

And the road from the shop
Is loaves, sugar, paraffin, newspapers, gossip.

Tinkers and shepherds
Have the whole round hill for a road.

Jesse Baggaley (1900-1976)

Born and raised in Lincoln. Wrote lyrics for folk songs including 'The Lincolnshire Shepherd'.

THE RESTLESS PEOPLE

Beyond the Heath are lowlands,
  behind the Wold is fen:
We've laboured here for one full year
  and now move on again.

For Ladyday[1] is flitting[2] time,
  and waggoners are few,
So my two sons and I we go
  to try a farm that's new.

We change and chop about a lot,
  from farm to farm we go;
And in a ten-mile ring there's not
  a farm we do not know.

There's not a field that's arable
  we've never ploughed or sown,
And we shall go from place to place
  until we own our own.

Aye, each year we shall flit again
  but know well in our hearts
We'll not go out our ten-mile ring,
  for those are foreign parts.

1. British name for festival of the Annunciation of the Virgin Mary. Until 1752 Lady Day was the beginning of the legal year; still a quarter day for rents or dues.
2. Changing one's abode.

Seamus Heaney (b.1939)

Irish poet. Educated at St Columb's College, Derry and Queen's University, Belfast where he became a lecturer. Later moved to Eire. Early poetry is rooted in the farmland of his youth.

CHURNING DAY

A thick crust, coarse-grained as limestone rough-cast,
hardened gradually on top of the four crocks
that stood, large pottery bombs, in the small pantry.
After the hot brewery of gland, cud and udder
cool porous earthenware fermented the buttermilk
for churning day, when the hooped churn was scoured
with plumping kettles and the busy scrubber
echoed daintily on the seasoned wood.
It stood then, purified, on the flagged kitchen floor.

Out came the four crocks, spilled their heavy lip
of cream, their white insides, into the sterile churn.
The staff, like a great whisky muddler fashioned
in deal wood, was plunged in, the lid fitted.
My mother took first turn, set up rhythms
that slugged and thumped for hours. Arms ached.
Hands blistered. Cheeks and clothes were spattered
with flabby milk.

             Where finally gold flecks
began to dance. They poured hot water then,
sterilized a birchwood-bowl
and little corrugated butter-spades.
Their short stroke quickened, suddenly
a yellow curd was weighting the churned up white,
heavy and rich, coagulated sunlight
that they fished, dripping, in a wide tin strainer,
heaped up like gilded gravel in the bowl.

The house would stink long after churning day
acrid as a sulphur mine. The empty crocks
were ranged along the wall again, the butter
in soft printed slabs was piled on pantry shelves.
And in the house we moved with gravid ease,
our brains turned crystals full of clean deal churns
the plash and gurgle of the sour-breathed milk,
the pat and slap of small spades on wet lumps.

Paul Coltman (b.1917)

Born in Maidstone. Studied English at St. John's, Oxford. Served with the Royal Artillery during World War II. Taught at Bradford and Steyning Grammar Schools.

OLD BIRD NAMES

Tom gave his spade a rest and watched:
Clatterdove and Chitty
Shufflewings and Cuddy.

Jack Shepherd heard them bawl their names:
Yafflebird and Pinker
Bogdrum and Boomer.

From dawn to dusk they helped Dick mow:
Puggy, Nun and Hedgepick,
Butcherbird and Bobbit.

Hodge knew them everyone by name:
Strumpydick and Chinky
Philip, Bob and Jenny.

The living wit of those old men:
Clodbird and Dapper,
Cuckoo's mate and Shriller.

A flutter of fading names:
Horselark and Pettychaps,
Barleybird and Wet-my-lips.

Barleybird: Whinchat	Chitty: Wren	Horselark: Corn Bunting	Shriller: Jay
Bob: Robin	Clatterdove: Woodpigeon	Jenny: Wren	Shufflewings: Hedge Sparrow
Bobbit: Robin	Clodbird: Corn Bunting	Nun: Blue Tit	Stumpdick: Wren
Bogdrum: Bittern	Cuckoo's mate: Wryneck	Pettychap: Blackcap	Wet-my-lips: Quail
Boomer: Bittern	Cuddy: Wren	Philip: House Sparrow	Yafflebird: Green Woodpecker
Butcherbird: Shrike	Dapper: Little Grebe	Pinker: Chaffinch	
Chinky: Chaffinch	Hedgepick: Hedge Sparrow	Puggy: Wren	

41

Heather Harrison (b.1943)

GREEN MAN[1]

Fleet in the forest,
leafshaken, wild in the wood,
flowers tousled in his hair,
garlanded with laurel and with ivy,
the Green Grotesque swoops out of stone and timber.
Locked in a church boss
his eyes start with alarm
at his enclosure. Brown priests agreed
to give his effigy a place.
That would bring the gaffers in,
the maids with May bandeaus,
the mothers full of fears and needing cures.

They could turn an eye
towards the old religion
while they received the new.
Christ nailed to a tree would keep their reverence
front facing; they could fringe
the altar of the new covenant with evergreen
with rosemary to sprig the nosegays left
under the wood-man's stare.
Needs are many and the winter cold,
best to placate all gods.
The Mediterranean Lord of Life
could promise them a warmer afterlife,
the Forest Sprite green leaves,
a yellow corn and a berried harvest.

---

1. In English folklore, an ancient forest god associated with the medieval festivities that celebrate the power of fertility and the arrival of spring (May Day). His face is often to be found in English church carvings in wood or stone; with a protruding tongue, leering expression and bulbous eyes. This ugly and malevolent icon needs propitiating perhaps by way of a toast. Hence our many pubs today named 'The Green Man'.

Bette McArdle (b.1935)

Born in Ayr. Now lives in Wick, Caithness. Was a freelance painter and journalist before turning to write poetry.

RURAL SCHOOL

ACKERGILL, CAITHNESS, APRIL NINETEEN-( )-SOMETHING

Pens stroke and scratch, dip in the china pots
that Phemie newly filled today; tight fingers
struggle, sweat, blot — the afternoon goes
slowly, drowsily measured by sliding spots
of sunlight across the pleats of my new
pinafore, down my button boots, leaping over teacher's
dais and up the varnished wall. Effie's
tongue, I know, is sliding out
for all I only see the fair springs
caught in gold about her cheek.
The schoolroom clock tocks heavy in the silence
in the silence, on the wall, securing us
to the earthbeat of the world's heart
in our carbolic coffin, brass-handled.
Something very important is a about to happen
or perhaps it is this moment, somehow
within time and us. Brilliant
beyond the window the road
runs all the way to Wick
or maybe further. It comes and goes and yet
is there. But not as green fields, patchwork
quilted, stay. The boys will take the road
to market, sea, to soldier, to be apprenticed
as watchmakers, coopers, masons, while we
marry and stitch the fields and fences in place.
Teacher, catching my eye,
frowns, checks his watch
linked by the albert[1]

43

on his dark serge breast,
pushes the spectacles up his nose
and notes his log: 'April 10 — The windows should be
         widened;
it is good for children to look out
upon roads and green fields.'

1. A short kind of watch chain named after Queen Victoria's husband.

44

Geoffrey K. Nelson

A sociologist as well as a poet. Has published books on social history, spiritualism and new religions. Two collections of poems include *To Be a Farmer's Boy*, published in 1993.

MUCK SPREADING

A warm job on a winter's day
is carting muck from the midden
up in waggons that bump and sway
along the wrinkled, rut sodden,
track, from par yard to fog swathed
fields, where the horses' hot breath steams
upon the silent mornings wreathed
air. While weeping from the dreaming
trees the grey skies drop their sorrow
in good hope of a fair morrow,

Now in the fields they spread the spoil
rich, ripe and odorous across
broad acres of the sleeping soil,
for on the farm there is no loss.
For from autumns lavish spending,
nought wasted, earth recycles all.
Spring bloom and summer fruit sending
and golden harvests in the Fall.

All throughout the year each
dying brings new life. See
where white fungi flourish
on that dead decaying tree.

Ann Taylor (1782-1866)

Ann and Jane Taylor were well known poem and hymn writers who lived in Colchester. Wrote the popular poem and nursery rhyme, 'Twinkle, twinkle, little star', published in 1806.

TURNIP TOPS

While yet the white frost sparkles over the ground,
And daylight just peeps from the misty blue sky,
In yonder green fields with my basket I'm found;
Come, buy my sweet turnip-tops – turnip-tops, buy!

Sadly cold are my fingers, all drenched with the dew,
For the sun has scarce risen the meadows to dry;
And my feet have got wet with a hole in my shoe,
Come haste, then, and buy my sweet turnip-tops buy!

While you are asleep, with your bed-curtains drawn,
On pillows of down, in your chambers so high,
I trip with the first rosy beam of the morn
To cull the green tops – come, my turnip-tops buy!

Robert Rendall (1898-1967)

Son of a master mariner. Born in Glasgow but spent most of his life on the Orkneys. Left school at 13 to help support the family after his father became ill. His interests included archaeology, theology, travel writing, natural history and marine biology; he was widely acknowledged as an expert on sea-shells. His deep personal faith in the creator God is evident in his poetry.

A COUNTRY BURIAL

A stranger in the parish
 I followed with the farm-folk
The upward-winding track
 between the winter fields,
And upon the hill-top
 stood among the mourners
Round the open grave
 in the still church-yard.

Distantly I heard
 the old prayer intoned,
Committing dust to dust,
 the soul to God Who gave,
But e'er a clod could fall
 in the grass-strewn grave
A sudden lark arose
 with a loud burst of singing.

I alone enraptured,
 saw the mounting bird
As if it were a spirit
 through the far clouds winging

Paul Coltman

PULBOROUGH OLD BRIDGE

I saw how they had set
the stone feet firm
in rock of the river's bed;
shaped buttresses to cleave
and throw aside
the worst onset
March could hurl at them:
barrelled four arches,
slate-smooth and bigger
for the middle spate.
how, respecting the river
and pitch of banks and slopes,
after consideration
of strength and safety,
they found it right to lay
the great grey stones
of the parapet,
so shaped to fit
man's being with the land
his mastery and respect.

PART TWO

A CELEBRATION

William Cowper (1731-1800)

Son of a rector, born in Great Berkhampstead, Herts. Called to the Bar in 1754. Suffered from depression. After recovery from a breakdown which led to suicide attempt, moved to Huntingdon and then Buckinghamshire where he was influenced by Evangelicals. Wrote hymns – 'God Moves in a Mysterious Way' and 'Oh For a Closer Walk with God'. Poems valued for their portraits of rural tranquillity.

from THE TASK
*(*THE WINTER WALK AT NOON*)*

> The Lord of all, Himself through all diffused,
> Sustains and is the life of all that lives.
> Nature is but a name for an effect
> Whose cause is God...

William Shakespeare (1564-1616)

Poet and playwright, born in Stratford-upon-Avon. Father was a glover, dealer in commodities, bailiff and JP. Married Anne Hathaway, eight years his senior; had a daughter and twins, Judith and Hamnet, who died aged 11. Worked in London at the Globe and Blackfriars theatres. Many of his plays were published posthumously.

from RICHARD II
(ACT II, SCENE I)

[GAUNT]
This royal throne of kings, this sceptred isle,
This earth of majesty, this seat of Mars,
This other Eden, demi-paradise,
This fortress built by Nature for herself
Against infection and the hand of war,
This happy breed of men, this little world,
This precious stone set in the silver sea,
Which serves it in the office of a wall,
Or as a moat defensive to a house
Against the envy of less happier lands;
This blessed plot, this earth, this realm, this England,
This nurse, this teeming womb of royal kings,
Feared by their breed and famous by their birth,
Renowned for their deeds as far from home
For Christian service and true chivalry
As is the sepulchre in stubborn Jewry
Of the world's ransom, blessed Mary's son;
This land of such dear souls, this dear dear land,
Dear for her reputation through the world,
Is now leased out—I die pronouncing it—
Like to a tenement or pelting farm.

Anon, Irish (9th Century)

A Meeting

The son of the King of the May
met a girl in green woods
on mid-summer's day
She gave him black fruit
from thorns
And the full of his arms
Of strawberries where they lay.

William Shakespeare

from THE WINTERS TALE
(ACT IV, SCENE IV)

[PERDITA]
...   —daffodils,
That come before the swallow dares, and take
The winds of March with beauty; violets, dim
But sweeter than the lids of Juno's[1] eyes
Or Cytherea's[2] breath; pale primroses,
That die unmarried ere they can behold
Bright Phoebus[3] in his strength—a malady
Most incident to maids; bold oxlips, and
The crown-imperial; lilies of all kinds,
The flower-de-luce being one.

1. Queen of Heaven, Roman Goddess.
2. Greek Goddess, also known as Aphrodite.
3. Greek Sun God, also called Apollo.

from A MIDSUMMER NIGHTS DREAM
(ACT II, SCENE I)

[OBERON]
I know a bank where the wild thyme blows,
Where oxlips and the nodding violet grows,
Quite over-canopied with luscious woodbine,
With sweet musk-roses, and with eglantine.
There sleeps Titania sometime of the night,
Lulled in these flowers with dances and delight;
And there the snake throws her enamelled skin,
Weed wide enough to wrap a fairy in...

John Milton (1608-1674)

Born in Bread Street, Cheapside; father was a scrivener and a musician. Went to Christ's College, Cambridge, where he began writing poetry in Latin, Italian and English. Spent years in political activity and defending religious, civil and domestic liberty. Married at 33 a wife of 17; they had three daughters and a son who died in infancy. Totally blind by 1652.

from PARADISE LOST
(BOOK IX)

As one who, long in populous city pent,
Where houses thick and sewers annoy the air,
Forth issuing on a summer's morn, to breathe
Among the pleasant villages and farms
Adjoined, from each thing met conceives delight,
The smell of grain, or tedded[1] grass, or kine,
Or dairy, each rural sight, each rural sound;
If chance with nymph-like step fair virgin pass,
What pleasing seemed, for her now pleases more,
She most, and in her looks sums all delight:
Such pleasure took the Serpent to behold
This flowery plat, the sweet recess of Eve
Thus early, thus alone...

1. Spread for drying.

Alfred, Lord Tennyson (1809-92)

Born in Somersby, Lincolnshire. Father was a rector. Studied at
Cambridge. Travelled with friend Arthur Hallam whose death he
immortalised in *In Memoriam*. Appointed Poet Laureate in 1850, year
of his marriage. T.S. Eliot called Tennyson 'a master of metric and
melancholia'.

from THE BROOK

I come from haunts of coot and hern,
   I make a sudden sally,
And sparkle out among the fern,
   To bicker down a valley.

By thirty hills I hurry down,
   Or slip between the ridges,
By twenty thorps, a little town,
   And half a hundred bridges.

Till last by Philip's farm I flow
   To join the brimming river,
For men may come and men may go,
   But I go on for ever.

I chatter over stony ways,
   In little sharps and trebles,
I bubble into eddying bays,
   I babble on the pebbles.

With many a curve my banks I fret,
   By many a field and fallow,
And many a fairy foreland set
   With willow-weed and mallow.

I chatter, chatter as I flow
   To join the brimming river,

For men may come and men may go
But I go on for ever.

I wind about, and in and out,
  With here a blossom sailing,
And here and there a lusty trout,
  And here and there a grayling;

And here and there a foamy flake
  Upon me, as I travel
With many a silvery water-break
  Above the golden gravel,

And draw them all along, and flow
  To join the brimming river,
For men may come and men may go
  But I go on for ever.

I steal by lawns and grassy plots,
  I slide by hazel covers;
I move the sweet forget-me-nots
  That grow for happy lovers.

I slip, I slide, I gloom, I glance,
  Among my skimming swallows;
I make the netted sunbeam dance
  Against my sandy shallows.

I murmur under moon and stars
  In brambly wildernesses;
I linger by my shingly bars,
  I loiter by my cresses;

And out again I curve and flow
  To join the brimming river,
For men may come and men may go
  But I go on for ever.

Thomas Hardy

THE YEAR'S AWAKENING

How do you know that the pilgrim track
Along the belting zodiac
Swept by the sun in his seeming rounds
Is traced by now to the Fishes' bounds
And into the Ram, when weeks of cloud
Have wrapt the sky in a clammy shroud,
And never as yet a tinct of spring
Has shown in the Earth's apparelling;
   O vespering bird, how do you know,
    How do you know?

How do you know, deep underground,
Hid in your bed from sight and sound,
Without a turn in temperature,
With weather life can scarce endure,
That light has won a fraction's strength,
And day put on some moments' length,
Wherof in merest rote will come,
Weeks hence, mild airs that do not numb;
   O crocus root, how do you know,
    How do you know?

Edward Thomas

THAW

Over the land freckled with snow half-thawed
The speculating rooks at their nests cawed
And saw from elm-tops, delicate as flower of grass,
What we below could not see, Winter pass.

A. E. Housman

'LOVELIEST OF TREES, THE CHERRY NOW'
(*from A SHROPSHIRE LAD*)

Loveliest of trees, the cherry now
Is hung with bloom along the bough,
And stands about the woodland ride
Wearing white for Eastertide.

Now, of my threescore years and ten,
Twenty will not come again,
And take from seventy springs a score,
It only leaves me fifty more.

And since to look at things in bloom
Fifty springs are little room,
About the woodlands I will go
To see the cherry hung with snow.

Gerard Manley Hopkins (1844-1889)

Born in Essex of High Anglican parents. Studied at Balliol, Oxford.
Influenced by Cardinal Newman. Became a Roman Catholic in 1866,
and joined the Jesuits two years later, when he symbolically burned
much of his early work. Ordained in 1877. Took chair of Greek and
Latin at University College, Dublin in 1884. Died of typhoid. Gained
spiritual insight from the natural world.

PIED BEAUTY

Glory be to God for dappled things —
      For skies of couple-colour as a brinded cow;
            For rose-moles all in stipple upon trout that swim;
Fresh-firecoal chestnut-falls; finches' wings;
      Landscape plotted and pieced — fold, fallow, and plough;
        And all trades, their gear and tackle and trim.

All things counter, original, spare, strange;
      Whatever is fickle, freckled (who knows how?)
        With swift, slow; sweet, sour; adazzle, dim;
He fathers-forth whose beauty is past change:
                     Praise him.

Lord Dunsany (1878-1957)

Edward John Moreton Drax Plunkett Dunsany, 18th baron, of Anglo-Irish parentage, lived in Wicklow. An essayist, novelist, short-story writer and poet. His dramatic work enjoys particular popularity in America.

SNOW ON THE EAST WIND

A black horse came to visit us,
   His hooves on the hills drumming
All the way from the Caucasus,
   And was three days coming.

On his back was a lady light,
   And cruelly did she ride him.
He dropped dead at our doors by night
   As she softly stepped from astride him.

Gerard Manley Hopkins

from SUNDRY FRAGMENTS AND IMAGES

(i)

The wind, that passes by so fleet,
Runs his fingers through the wheat,
And leaves the blades, where'er he will veer,
Tingling between dusk and silver.

(iv)

There is an island, wester'd in the main,
Around it balances the level sea.

(v)

The time was late and the wet yellow woods
Told off their leaves along the piercing gale...

Alfred, Lord Tennyson

Song

I

A spirit haunts the year's last hours
Dwelling amid these yellowing bowers.
　　　To himself he talks;
For at eventide, listening earnestly,
At his work you may hear him sob and sigh
　　　In the walks;
　Earthward he boweth the heavy stalks
Of the mouldering flowers.
　　　Heavily hangs the broad sunflower
　　　　Over its grave i' the earth so chilly;
　　　Heavily hangs the hollyhock,
　　　　Heavily hangs the tiger-lily.

II

The air is damp, and hush'd, and close,
As a sick man's room when he taketh repose
　　　An hour before death;
My very heart faints and my whole soul grieves
At the moist rich smell of the rotting leaves,
　　　And the breath
　Of the fading edges of box beneath,
And the year's last rose.
　　　Heavily hangs the broad sunflower
　　　　Over its grave i' the earth so chilly;
　　　Heavily hangs the hollyhock,
　　　　Heavily hangs the tiger-lily.

William Butler Yeats (1865-1939)

Son of the celebrated Dublin painter, John B. Yeats. Studied art but abandoned it for literature at 21. Founded the Irish Literary Society in London, 1892, and (with others) the Irish National Theatre in Dublin, 1904. Ardent Irish nationalist. Received the Nobel Prize for literature in 1923.

THE FALLING OF THE LEAVES

Autumn is over the long leaves that love us,
And over the mice in the barley sheaves;
Yellow the leaves of the rowan above us,
And yellow the wet wild-strawberry leaves.

The hour of the waning of love has beset us,
And weary and worn are our sad souls now;
Let us part, ere the season of passion forget us,
With a kiss and a tear on thy drooping brow.

A. E. Housman

'ON WENLOCK EDGE THE WOOD'S IN TROUBLE'
(*from A SHROPSHIRE LAD*)

On Wenlock Edge the wood's in trouble,
His forest fleece the Wrekin heaves;
The gale, it plies the saplings double,
And thick on Severn snow the leaves.

'Twould blow like this through holt and hanger
When Uricon[1] the city stood:
'Tis the old wind in the old anger,
But then it threshed another wood.

Then, 'twas before my time, the Roman
At yonder heaving hill would stare:
The blood that warms an English yeoman,
The thoughts that hurt him, they were there.

There, like the wind through woods in riot,
Through him the gale of life blew high;
The tree of man was never quiet:
Then 'twas the Roman, now 'tis I.

The gale, it plies the saplings double,
It blows so hard, 'twill soon be gone;
To-day the Roman and his trouble
Are ashes under Uricon.

1. The Roman Station Uriconium on the site of Wroxeter in Shropshire applied to apparently Pre-Cambrian igneous rocks forming the Wrekin.

Walter de la Mare (1873-1956)

Born in Kent of well-to-do parents. Joined an oil company aged 16 where he worked for twenty years. Wrote poetry for adults and children, often with undercurrent of melancholy. Buried in St. Paul's Cathedral.

ALL THAT'S PAST

Very old are the woods;
  And the buds that break
Out of the brier's boughs,
  When March winds wake,
So old with their beauty are —
  Oh, no man knows
Through what wild centuries
  Roves back the rose.

Very old are the brooks;
  And the rills that rise
Where snow sleeps cold beneath
  The azure skies
Sing such a history
  Of come and gone,
Their every drop is as wise
  As Solomon.

Very old are we men;
  Our dreams are tales
Told in dim Eden
  By Eve's nightingales;
We wake and whisper awhile,
  But, the day gone by,
Silence in sleep like fields
  Of amaranth lie.

Alfred, Lord Tennyson

from TITHONUS

The woods decay, the woods decay and fall,
The vapours weep their burthen to the ground,
Man comes and tills the field and lies beneath,
And after many a summer dies the swan.
Me only cruel immortality
Consumes; I wither slowly in thine arms,
Here at the quiet limit of the world,
A white-hair'd shadow roaming like a dream
The ever silent spaces of the East,
Far-folded mists, and gleaming halls of morn.

Frances Cornford (1886-1960)

The grand-daughter of Charles Darwin, she was born in Cambridge and spent most of her life in that area.

THE COAST: NORFOLK

As on the highway's quiet edge
He mows the grass beside the hedge,
The old man has for company
The distant, grey, salt-smelling sea,
A poppied field, a cow and calf,
The finches on the telegraph.

Across his faded back a hone,
He slowly, slowly scythes alone
In silence of the wind-soft air,
With ladies' bedstraw everywhere,
With whitened corn, and tarry[1] poles,
And far-off gulls like risen souls.

1. Telegraph poles.

Saunders Lewis (1893-1985)

A great figure in twentieth century Welsh literature. Born in Wallasey, Cheshire, of two generations of Calvinist Methodist ministers.

ASCENSION THURSDAY
Translated by Gwyn Thomas

What's on this May morning in the hills?
Look at them, at the gold of the broom and laburnum
And the bright surplice on the shoulders of the thorn
And the intent emerald of the grass and the still calves;

See the candlestick of the chestnut tree alight,
The groves kneeling and the mute birch a nun,
The cuckoo's two-notes over the shining hush of the brook
And the form of the mist bending from the censer of the meadows:

Come out, you men, from the council houses before
The rabbits scamper, come with the weasel to see
The elevation of the unblemished host
And the Father kissing the Son in the white dew.

Original Welsh
Difiau Dyrchafael

Beth sydd ymlaen fore o Fai ar y bronnydd?
Edrychwch arnynt, ar aur y banadl a'r euron
A'r wenwisg loyw ar ysgwyddau'r ddraenen
Ac emrallt astud y gwellt a'r lloi llonydd;

Gwelwch ganhwyllbren y gastanwydden yn olau,
Y perthi'n penlinio a'r lleian fedwen fud,
Deunod y gog dros ust llathraid y ffrwd
A'r rhith tarth yn gwyro o thuser y dolau:

Dowch allan, ddynion, o'r tai cyngor cyn
Gwasgar y cwning, dowch gyda'r wenci i weled
Codi o'r ddaear afrlladen ddifrycheulyd
A'r Tad yn cusanu'r Mab yn y gwlith gwyn.

Peter Russell (b.1921)

Born in Bristol. Served in 1939-46 with British Indian Army. Owner of publishing house, Pound Press. Lived in Venice, 1965-83. Poet-in-residence at University of Victoria, British Columbia and Purdue University, Indiana. Teaching Fellow at the Imperial Iranian Academy of Philosophy, Tehran, 1977-79. Lives in Arezzo, Italy.

from MNEMOSYNE

I stand aside to let the seasons pass

And ecstasy, that threads like pearls
Our origins and presences and ends
Is like the first wild jonquils of the spring
That shimmer in the wind and sun
Upon a lonely island no one knows
Drawing the swallow transports out of Africa

And every clod and every grain of quartz
Gleams like the infinite stars
Answering around the universe

Laurie Lee (1914-1997)

Born in Gloucestershire, educated at Slad Village School and Stroud Central School. Travelled around Europe, 1935-39. Worked for the Ministry of Information as publications editor during World War II. Wrote novels, screenplays and travel books as well as poetry.

DAY OF THESE DAYS

Such a morning it is when love
leans through geranium windows
and calls with a cockerel's tongue.

When red-haired girls scamper like roses
over the rain-green grass,
and the sun drips honey.

When the hedgerows grow venerable,
berries dry black as blood,
and holes suck in their bees.

Such a morning it is when mice
run whispering from the church,
dragging dropped ears of harvest.

When the partridge draws back his spring
and shoots like a buzzing arrow
over the grained and mahogany fields.

When no table is bare,
and no breast dry,
and the tramp feeds of ribs of rabbit.

Such a day it is when time
piles up the hills like pumpkins,
and the streams run golden.

When all men smell good,
and the cheeks of girls
are as baked bread to the mouth.

As bread and beanflowers
the touch of their lips,
and their white teeth sweeter than cucumbers.

Dylan Thomas (1914-53)

Born in Swansea. Educated at the local grammar school, where his father taught English. Began writing poetry at school. Worked as a journalist, then moved to London in 1934 and worked as a scriptwriter and broadcaster for the BBC. Returned to live in Wales with his wife, Caitlin Macnamara, in 1949. Also wrote short stories and essays. Died of alcoholic poisoning while visiting the USA.

FERN HILL

Now as I was young and easy under the apple boughs
About the lilting house and happy as the grass was green,
   The night above the dingle starry,
    Time let me hail and climb
   Golden in the heydays of his eyes,
And honoured among wagons I was prince of the apple towns
And once below a time I lordly had the trees and leaves
    Trail with daises and barley
   Down the rivers of the windfall light.

And as I was green and carefree, famous among the barns
About the happy yard and singing as the farm was home,
   In the sun that is young once only,
    Time let me play and be
   Golden in the mercy of his means,
And green and golden I was huntsman and herdsman, the calves
Sang to my horn, the foxes on the hills barked clear and cold,
    And the sabbath rang slowly
   In the pebbles of the holy streams.

All the sun long it was running, it was lovely, the hay
Fields high as the house, the tunes from the chimneys, it was air
   And playing, lovely and watery
    And fire green as grass.
    And nightly under the simple stars
As I rode to sleep the owls were bearing the farm away,

All the moon long I heard, blessed among the stables, the nightjars
    Flying with the ricks, and the horses
        Flashing into the dark.

And then to awake, and the farm, like a wanderer white
With the dew, come back, the cock on his shoulder: it was all
    Shining, it was Adam and maiden,
        The sky gathered again
    And the sun grew round that very day.
So it must have been after the birth of the simple light
In the first, spinning place, the spellbound horses walking warm
    Out of the whinnying green stable
        On to the fields of praise.

And honoured among foxes and pheasants by the gay house
Under the new made clouds and happy as the heart was long,
    In the sun born over and over,
        I ran my heedless ways,
    My wishes raced through the house high hay
And nothing I cared, at my sky blue trades, that time allows
In all his tuneful turning so few and such morning songs
    Before the children green and golden
        Follow him out of grace,

Nothing I cared, in the lamb white days, that time would take me
Up to the swallow thronged loft by the shadow of my hand,
    In the moon that is always rising,
        Nor that riding to sleep
    I should hear him fly with the high fields
And wake to the farm forever fled from the childless land.
Oh as I was young and easy in the mercy of his means,
        Time held me green and dying
    Though I sang in my chains like the sea.

George Barker (1913-91)

Born in Essex. Irish mother. Taught in universities in Japan and the USA. Lived in the USA and Canada, 1940-43. Also wrote essays and novels. *Calamiterror*, written in 1937, was inspired by the Spanish Civil War.

from CALAMITERROR
(PART II)

This is that hank of hair and raw bone
That frequently in remote places
The cottagers find caught in trees.
This is the weasel suspended from bush branch,
The adder glistening in the noose of string
Seen in the Worcester lane; the head of eel
Blocking the water system. Thus god's engine
Ejects its refuse.

Ted Hughes (1930-2000)

Born in Yorkshire. As a boy spent much time fishing and shooting. Met his future wife, Sylvia Plath, at Cambridge. First collection of poems published in 1957. Appointed Poet Laureate in 1984. Also wrote plays for children and adults. His poetry reflects the brutal aspects of nature.

PENNINES IN APRIL

If this county were a sea (that is solid rock
Deeper than any sea) these hills heaving
Out of the east, mass behind mass, at this height
Hoisting heather and stones to the sky
Must burst upwards and topple into Lancashire.

Perhaps, as the earth turns, such ground-stresses
Do come rolling westward through the locked land.
Now, measuring the miles of silence
Your eye takes the strain: through

Landscapes gliding blue as water
Those barrellings of strength are heaving slowly and heave
To your feet and surf upwards
In a still, fiery air, hauling the imagination,
Carrying the larks upward.

Herbert Williams (b.1932)

Born in Aberystwyth; spent most of his life in Cardiff. Fellow of the
Welsh Academy. Radio producer, journalist, freelance writer and
broadcaster, novelist and poet.

A CELEBRATION

You will know it, the ragwort,
Though not perhaps by name—
A yellow flower, full
Of mischief for the gardener.
A common weed, populous
As common people, and as apt
To make the best of an indifferent lot.
You will know its pertinacious ways.
Its bland possession of a tumbled soil,
And you will wonder why
I celebrate its impudence.

Well, I will tell you. There is a spot
In Cardiff where the Taff
Flows between grubby banks. The view
Is nonexistent. Concrete, bricks.
And traffic brash as pain.
Between the road and river runs
A row of rusty railings. And just here
The ragwort grows. A common weed.
But such a blaze of beauty that it blooms
Redemption on the urban blasphemy,
And justifies itself like Magdalene.

Stephen Spender (1909-95)

Son of a distinguished journalist. Brought up in Hampstead. Left
Oxford without a degree and lived in Germany for a while. Lived in
Spain during the Civil War, supporting the Republicans. Served as a
fireman in London during the Second World War. Held many academic
posts, including a professorship of English at University College,
London, 1970-75. Awarded a knighthood in 1983.

THE CHALK BLUE BUTTERFLY

The Chalk Blue (clinging to
A harebell stem, where it loops
Its curving wirefine neck
From which there hangs the flowerbell
Shaken by the wind that shakes
Too, the butterfly)—
Opens now, now shuts, its wings,
Opening, shutting, on a hinge
Sprung at touch of sun or shadow.
   Open, the sunned wings mirror
Minute, double, all the sky.
   Shut, the ghostly underwing
Is cloud-opaque, bordered by
Copper spots embossed
By a pigmy hammering.

   I look and look, as though my eyes
Could hold the Chalk Blue in a vice,
Waiting for some other witness
— That child's blue gaze, miraculous.
But today I am alone.

Kathleen Raine (b.1908)

Born in Essex, with a Scottish mother and a Northumbrian father. Her poetry is inspired by landscapes of Scotland, particularly Wester Ross. Has published criticism and autobiography as well as poetry.

CHILDHOOD

I see all, am all, all.
I leap along the line of the horizon hill,
I am a cloud in the high sky,
I trace the veins of intricate fern.
In the dark ivy wall the wren's world
Soft to bird breast nest of round eggs is mine,
Mine in the rowan-tree the blackbird's thought
Inviolate in leaves ensphered.
I am bird-world, leaf-life, I am wasp-world hung
Under low berry-branch of hidden thorn,
Friable paper-world humming with hate,
Moss-thought, rain-thought, stone still thought on the hill.

Never, never, never will I go home to be a child.

Charles L. Graves

Born in 1856. The brother of Alfred Perceval Graves, who was president of the Irish Literary Society and the author of many songs and ballads. Charles was educated at Marlborough and at Christ Church, Oxford. Became well known as a journalist and as a music critic. Author of several books on music and musicians, he also wrote parodies and skits in prose and verse.

NORFOLK: A STUDY IN COUNTRY CHARACTERISTICS

Norfolk, although no mountain ranges
    Girdle your plains with a bastioned height,
Yet is your landscape rich in changes,
    Filling the eye with delight -
Heath-clad uplands and lonely dingles,
    Slow streams stealing through level meads.
Flats where the marsh with the ocean mingles,
    Meres close guarded by sentinel reeds.

Never a mile but some church-tower hoary
    Stands for a witness, massive and tall,
How men furthered God's greater glory -
    Blakeney and Cley and Salle.
Never a village but in its borders
    Signs of a stormy past remain,
Walls that were manned by Saxon warders,
    Barrows that guard the bones of the Dane.

Deep in your heart Rome left her traces,
    Normans held your manors in fee,
Italy lent you her southern graces,
    Dutchmen bridled your sea.
Flemings wove you their silks and woollens,
    Romany magic still to you clings,
And the fairest daughter of all the Bullens[1]
    Blent your blood with that of your Kings.

Yours are the truest names in England -
    Overy Staithe and Icknield Way,
Waveney River, Ringmere and Ringland,
    Wymondham and Wormegay.
Land of windmills and brown-winged wherries,
    Gliding along with the gait of Queens;
Land of the Broads, the dykes, and the ferries,
    Land of the sounds, the brecks, the denes.[2]

Gipsy lore, the heart of his stories,
    Borrow[3] gleaned in his Norwich home.
Broadland, aflame with sunset glories,
    Fired the vision of Crome.[4]
Tombland's echo throughout the pages
    Of Browne[5] like a stately Requiem runs;
Nelson, 'a name to resound for ages,'
    Crowns the roll of your hero sons.

1. Anne Boleyn - second wife of Henry VIII and eldest daughter of Sir Thomas Bullen of
Blickling.
2. Dunes.
3. George Borrow (1805-81). Born East Dereham. Expert on gypsy lore.
4. John Crome (1768-1821). Son of Norwich weaver. Founded Norwich school of painting.
5. Sir Thomas Browne (1605-82). Distinguished doctor and writer who settled in Norwich.
Knighted by King Charles II.

Edward Thomas

THE PATH

Running along a bank, a parapet
That saves from the precipitous wood below
The level road, there is a path. It serves
Children for looking down the long smooth steep,
Between the legs of beech and yew, to where
A fallen tree checks the sight: while men and women
Content themselves with the road and what they see
Over the bank, and what the children tell.
The path, winding like silver, trickles on,
Bordered and even invaded by thinnest moss
That tries to cover roots and crumbling chalk
With gold, olive, and emerald, but in vain.
The children wear it. They have flattened the bank
On top, and silvered it between the moss
With the current of their feet, year after year.
But the road is houseless, and leads not to school.
To see a child is rare there, and the eye
Has but the road, the wood that overhangs
And underyawns it, and the path that looks
As if it led on to some legendary
Or fancied place where men have wished to go
And stay; till, sudden, it ends where the wood ends.

Ted Hughes

FERN

Here is the fern's frond, unfurling a gesture,
Like a conductor whose music will now be pause
And the one note of silence
To which the whole earth dances gravely.

The mouse's ear unfurls its trust,
The spider takes up her bequest,
And the retina
Reins the creation with a bridle of water.

And, among them, the fern
Dances gravely, like the plume
Of a warrior returning, under the low hills,

Into his own kingdom.

Harold Massingham (b.1932)

Born in South Yorkshire. Went to Manchester University. Won the Cholmondley Award for poetry in 1968.

STICKLEBACK

Male, pale blue, in quietude -
a bacillus in lymph -

with kidney-glue, a bodkin-skill
among sprig-weedy oddments,

makes his tubular nest. Then woos
his world, polygamist

of the pond; coercive,
vicious in rivalry,

rounding up fish-wives
efficiently, in-and-out of horn-

wort, and with no credentials
but his silvery belly's

phosphor of blood. Later,
as at a fabulous den, takes

custody of a generation,
fry for survival, the family-name.

Margaret Buckle

Blind poet and song writer of the Yorkshire Dales; recently the subject of a Yorkshire TV documentary.

THE OLD THORN

See where he stands, not tall,
           but squat and strong,
His score of stems, his myriad branches armed
With black sharp thorns. His gnarly,
           riven bark,
Harsh-angled twigs and stiffly-moving limbs
Tell of grim winters, grim tenacity.
See where his roots go down. They broke the rock
On which he, seedling, grew. The limestone block
Split at his iron thrust, and down he went
Into the scanty soil, but still held fast
The shattered fragments of the crumbling stone,
And sucks the substance of the rock itself.
Year after year, he craves, and thrusts
           and strives,
Holds fast all that he has, gives nothing back,
But eats the very leaves from his own boughs
In passionate desire to grow and live.

But then comes Spring, and like some
           stern old saint,
Amazed, in Heaven, to feel his robes and crown,
The dark, rough thorn is clothed
           in milk-white blossom,
Feels all his substance change with
           mounting life,
And sets his seeds of immortality.

Ted Hughes

THISTLES

Against the rubber tongues of cows and the hoeing hands of men
Thistles spike the summer air
Or crackle open under a blue-black pressure.

Every one a revengeful burst
Of resurrection, a grasped fistful
Of splintered weapons and Icelandic frost thrust up

From the underground stain of a decayed Viking.
They are like pale hair and the gutturals of dialects.
Every one manages a plume of blood.

Then they grow grey, like men.
Mown down, it is a feud. Their sons appear,
Stiff with weapons, fighting back over the same ground.

George Szirtes (b.1948)

Born in Budapest, Hungary. Came to England in 1956. Lecturer and translator. Currently living in Wymondham, Norfolk.

CHILDREN BY THE RIVER

The duck-scrum at the pond's edge
Narrows about a star of bread
Thrown careless on grey heaps of water

Clang clang go the bells
Their rapid notes tossed against the branches.
Birds peeling from the bank —

Older pictures show how the scene looked
To a disciple of Palmer[1] — dark and gold
And haloed in broad leaves, a shepherd.

And from those trees a bull emerging
Grecian and lust eaten, hooting for his cow
Who lies beyond the hedges sleeping.

1. Samuel Palmer.

Rupert Brooke (1887-1915)

Born in Rugby. Educated at Rugby School where his father was a master and at King's College, Cambridge. A nervous breakdown in 1913 led him to travel to USA, Canada and the Pacific. Joined RNVR in 1914 and took part in the Antwerp expedition. Died of blood poisoning en route to the Dardanelles.

THE OLD VICARAGE, GRANTCHESTER
(Café des Westens, Berlin, May 1912)

Just now the lilac is in bloom,
All before my little room;
And in my flower-beds, I think,
Smile the carnation and the pink;
And down the borders, well I know,
The poppy and the pansy blow...
Oh! there the chestnuts, summer through,
Beside the river make for you
A tunnel of green gloom, and sleep
Deeply above; and green and deep
The stream mysterious glides beneath,
Green as a dream and deep as death.
—Oh, damn! I know it! and I know
How the May fields all golden show,
And when the day is young and sweet,
Gild gloriously the bare feet
That run to bathe...
Du lieber Gott!

Here am I, sweating, sick, and hot,
And there the shadowed waters fresh
Lean up to embrace the naked flesh.
Temperamentvoll German Jews
Drink beer around;—and *there* the dews

90

Are soft beneath a morn of gold.
Here tulips bloom as they are told;
Unkempt about those hedges blows
An English unofficial rose;
And there the unregulated sun
Slopes down to rest when day is done,
And wakes a vague unpunctual star,
A slippered Hesper; and there are
Meads towards Haslingfield and Coton
Where *das Betreten*'s not *verboten*.

ειθε γενοιμην....would I were
In Grantchester, in Grantchester!—
Some, it may be, can get in touch
With Nature there, or Earth, or such.
And clever modern men have seen
A Faun a-peeping through the green,
And felt the Classics were not dead,
To glimpse a Naiad's reedy head,
Or hear the Goat-foot piping low:...
But these are things I do not know.
I only know that you may lie
Day long and watch the Cambridge sky,
And, flower-lulled in sleepy grass,
Hear the cool lapse of hours pass,
Until the centuries blend and blur
In Grantchester, in Grantchester...
Still in the dawnlit waters cool
His ghostly Lordship swims his pool,
And tries the strokes, essays the tricks,
Long learnt on Hellespont, or Styx.
Dan Chaucer hears his river still
Chatter beneath a phantom mill.
Tennyson notes, with studious eye,
How Cambridge waters hurry by...
And in that garden, black and white,
Creep whispers through the grass all night;

And spectral dance, before the dawn,
A hundred Vicars down the lawn;
Curates, long dust, will come and go
On lissom, clerical, printless toe;
And oft between the boughs is seen
The sly shade of a Rural Dean...
Till, at a shiver in the skies,
Vanishing with Satanic cries,
The prim ecclesiastic rout
Leaves but a startled sleeper-out,
Grey heavens, the first bird's drowsy calls,
The falling house that never falls.

God ! I will pack, and take a train,
And get me to England once again!
For England's the one land, I know,
Where men with Splendid Hearts may go;
And Cambridgeshire, of all England,
The shire for Men who Understand;
And of *that* district I prefer
The lovely hamlet Grantchester.
For Cambridge people rarely smile,
Being urban, squat, and packed with guile;
And Royston men in the far South
Are black and fierce and strange of mouth;
At Over they fling oaths at one,
And worse than oaths at Trumpington,
And Ditton girls are mean and dirty,
And there's none in Harston under thirty,
And folks in Shelford and those parts
Have twisted lips and twisted hearts,
And Barton men make Cockney rhymes,
And Coton's full of nameless crimes,
And things are done you'd not believe
At Madingley, on Christmas Eve.
Strong men have run for miles and miles,
When one from Cherry Hinton smiles;

Strong men have blanched, and shot their wives,
Rather than send them to St Ives;
Strong men have cried like babes, bydam,
To hear what happened at Babraham.
But Grantchester! ah, Grantchester!
There's peace and holy quiet there,
Great clouds along pacific skies,
And men and women with straight eyes,
Lithe children lovelier than a dream,
A bosky wood, a slumbrous stream,
And little kindly winds that creep
Round twilight corners, half asleep.
In Grantchester their skins are white;
They bathe by day, they bathe by night;
The women there do all they ought;
The men observe the Rules of Thought.
They love the Good; they worship Truth;
They laugh uproariously in youth;
(And when they get to feeling old,
They up and shoot themselves, I'm told)...

Ah God! to see the branches stir
Across the moon at Grantchester!
To smell the thrilling-sweet and rotten
Unforgettable, unforgotten
River-smell, and hear the breeze
Sobbing in the little trees.
Say, do the elm-clumps greatly stand
Still guardians of that holy land?
The chestnuts shade, in reverend dream,
The yet unacademic stream?
Is dawn a secret shy and cold
Anadyomene, silver-gold?
and sunset still a golden sea
From Haslingfield to Madingley?
And after, ere the night is born,
Do hares come out about the corn?

Oh, is the water sweet and cool,
Gentle and brown, above the pool?
And laughs the immortal river still
Under the mill, under the mill?
Say, is there Beauty yet to find?
And Certainty? and Quiet kind?
Deep meadows yet, for to forget
The lies, and truths, and pain?...oh! yet
Stands the Church clock at ten to three?
And is there honey still for tea?

Cecil Day-Lewis (1904-72)

Born in Eire, son of a Church of Ireland minister. Family moved to England. Educated at Sherborne School and Wadham College, Oxford. Worked as a teacher until 1935. Active in the Communist Party for three years in the thirties, but turned from political to personal and pastoral themes in later years. Appointed Poet Laureate in 1968.

from REQUIEM FOR THE LIVING

SANCTUS

Holy this earth where unamazed we dwell –
Mothering earth, our food, our fabulous well –
A mote in space, a flicker of time's indifferent wheel.

Holy the marigold play of evening sun
On wall and tree, the dawn's light-fingered run,
Night's muted strings, the shimmering chords of summer noon.

Holy the salmon leaping up a fall,
Leopard's glide, birds and bees their seasonal
Employ, the shy demeanour of antelope and snail.

Praise wild, tame, common, rare – chrysanthemums
That magnify a back-yard in the slums.
Gentian and passion flower, primrose of deep combes.

Praise the white orchards of the cloudful west,
Wheat prairies with abundance in their breast,
The seas, the mineral mountains, the jungle and the waste.

Holy the flowering of our genial dust
In art, law, science, raising from earth's crust
A testament of vision made good and truth diffused.

Holy the climber's grit, the athlete's grace,
Whippets unleashed and pigeons' homing race,
A stadium's roar, a theatre's hush – they also praise.

Oh praise man's mind that, questioning why things are
And whence, haloes the moon with a new star,
Peers into nature's heart and cons the order there.

Oh praise what makes us creatures breed and build
Over death's void, and know ourselves fulfilled
In that age-hallowed trinity – man, woman, child.

Holy the heights where flesh and spirit wed.
Holy this earth, our source, our joy, our bread.
Holy to praise man's harvest and treasure his brave seed.

PART THREE
DESTRUCTION

Jorge Luis Borges (1899-1986)

Born in Buenos Aires. Educated in Europe. Director of the National Library of Buenos Aires, 1955-1973. Internationally renowned as a poet, essayist and short story writer.

from PARADISO, XXXI, 108

> ...who of us has never felt, while walking through the twilight or writing a date from his past, that something infinite had been lost?

Anon (Early 17th Century)

'A SPARROW-HAWK PROUD'

A sparrow-hawk proud did hold in wicked jail
Music's sweet chorister, the nightingale;
To whom with sighs she said, 'O set me free,
And in my song I'll praise no bird but thee'.
The hawk replied, 'I will not lose my diet
To let a thousand such enjoy their quiet'.

William Wordsworth (1770-1850)

Born in Cumbria, the son of an attorney. Lost both parents by the age of 13. Studied at St John's, Cambridge. Spent time in France where he was inspired by the Revolution. Lived with sister Dorothy in Dorset and Somerset. In 1802 married Mary who bore him five children. Appointed Stamp Distributor for Westmorland in 1813, where he spent the rest of his life having abandoned the radical politics of his youth. Became Poet Laureate in 1843.

from THE EXCURSION
(BOOK VIII - THE PARSONAGE)

'Meanwhile, at social Industry's command,
How quick, how vast an increase! From the germ
Of some poor hamlet, rapidly produced
Here a huge town, continuous and compact,
Hiding the face of earth for leagues—and there,
Where not a habitation stood before,
Abodes of men irregularly massed
Like trees in forests,—spread through spacious tracts,
O'er which the smoke of unremitting fires
Hangs permanent, and plentiful as wreaths
Of vapour glittering in the morning sun.
And, wheresoe'er the traveller turns his steps,
He sees the barren wilderness erased.
Or disappearing; triumph that proclaims
How much the mild Directress of the plough
Owes to alliance with these new-born arts!...'

William Cowper

THE POPLAR-FIELD

The poplars are fell'd, farewell to the shade
And the whispering sound of the cool colonnade,
The winds play no longer, and sing in the leaves,
Nor Ouse on his bosom their image receives.

Twelve years have elaps'd since I first took a view
Of my favourite field and the bank where they grew,
And now in the grass behold they are laid,
And the tree is my seat that once lent me a shade.

The blackbird has fled to another retreat
Where the hazels afford him a screen from the heat,
And the scene where his melody charm'd me before
Resounds with his sweet-flowing ditty no more.

My fugitive years are all hasting away,
And I must ere long lie as lowly as they,
With a turf on my breast, and a stone at my head,
Ere another such grove shall arise in its stead.

'Tis a sight to engage me, if any thing can,
To muse on the perishing pleasures of man;
Though his life be a dream, his enjoyments, I see,
Have a being less durable even than he.

John Clare

The Lament of Swordy Well

I'm Swordy Well, a piece of land
    That's fell upon the town,
Who worked me till I couldn't stand
    And crush me now I'm down.

There was a time my bit of ground
    Made freeman of the slave,
The ass no pounder'd dare to pound
    When I his supper gave.

The gipsy's camp was not afraid,
    I made his dwelling free,
Till vile enclosure came, and made
    A parish slave of me.

Alas, dependence, thou'rt a brute
    Want only understands;
His feelings wither branch and root
    Who falls in parish hands.

The muck that clouts the ploughman's shoe,
    The moss that hides the stone,
Now I'm become the parish due,
    Is more than I can own.

The silver springs are naked dykes,
    With scarce a clump of rushes;
When gain got nigh, the tasteless tykes
    Grubbed up trees, banks, and bushes.

Though I'm no man, yet any wrong
    Some sort of right may seek,
And I am glad if e'en a song
    Give me the room to speak.

I've got among such grubbling gear
    And such a hungry pack,
If I brought harvests twice a year,
    They'd bring me nothing back.

And should the price of grain get high
    —Lord help and keep it low!—
I shan't possess a butterfly
    Nor get a weed to grow,

I shan't possess a yard of ground
    To bid a mouse to thrive;
For gain has put me in a pound,
    I scarce can keep alive.

Ah me!—they turned me inside out
    For sand and grit and stones,
And turned my old green hills about
    And picked my very bones.

The bees fly round in feeble rings
    And find no blossom by,
Then thrum their almost weary wings
    Upon the moss, and die.

Rabbits that find my hills turned o'er
    Forsake my poor abode;
They dread a workhouse like the poor,
    And nibble on the road.

If with a clover bottle now
    Spring dares to lift her head,
The next day brings the hasty plough
    And makes me misery's bed.

I've scarce a nook to call my own
    For things that creep or fly;
The beetle hiding 'neath a stone
    Does well to hurry by.

And if I could but find a friend
    With no deceit to sham,
Who'd send me some few sheep to tend,
    And leave me as I am,

To keep my hills from cart and plough
    And strife of mongrel men,
And as spring found me find me now,
    I should look up agen.

And save his Lordship's woods, that past
    The day of danger dwell,
Of all the fields I am the last
    That my own face can tell;

Yet what with stone-pits' delving holes,
    And strife to buy and sell,
My name will quickly be the whole
    That's left of Swordy Well.

David Herbert Lawrence (1885-1930)

Novelist, short-story writer, essayist, critic, playwright and poet. One of five children of a Nottinghamshire miner. After leaving school became a junior clerk. Went to Nottingham University to train in teaching. Worked as a teacher in London. In 1912 met Frieda and eloped to Germany. Classed as unfit for military service; spent war years in Cornwall until accused of spying for the Germans. *The Rainbow* banned on grounds of obscenity. Disillusioned by England, left in 1922 for world-wide travels. Died of tubercolosis in France.

from NOTTINGHAM AND THE MINING COUNTRY

The real tragedy of England, as I see it, is the tragedy of ugliness. The country is so lovely: the man-made England is so vile. I know that the ordinary collier, when I was a boy, had a peculiar sense of beauty, coming from his intuitive and instinctive consciousness, which was awakened down pit. And the fact that he met with just cold ugliness and raw materialism when he came up into daylight, and particularly when he came to the Square or the Breach, and to his own table, killed something in him, and in a sense spoiled him as a man. The woman almost invariably nagged about material things. She was taught to do it; she was encouraged to do it. It was a mother's business to see that her son 'got on', and it was the man's business to provide the money. In my father's generation, with the old wild England behind them, and the lack of education, the man was not beaten down. But in my generation, the boys I went to school with, colliers now, have all been beaten down, what with the din-din-dinning of Board Schools, books, cinemas, clergymen, the whole national and human consciousness hammering on the fact of material prosperity above all things...

Wilfred Wilson Gibson (1878-1962)

Born in Hexham, Northumberland. The First World War inspired short war poems, but much of his verse speaks of northern rural themes.

FIRE

Across the Cleveland countryside the train
Panted and jolted through the lurid night
Of monstrous slag-heaps in the leaping light
Of belching furnaces: the driving rain
Lacing the glass with gold in that red glare
That momently revealed the cinderous land
Of blasted fields, that stretched out on either hand,
With livid waters gleaming here and there.

By hovels of men who labour till they die
With iron and with the fire that never sleeps,
We plunged in pitchy night among huge heaps -
Then once again that red glare lit the sky,
And high above the highest hill of slag
I saw Prometheus[1] hanging from his crag.

---

1. According to legend, Prometheus stole fire from the gods; so Zeus chained him to a rock on Mount Caucasus, where in the daytime an eagle ate his liver which was restored each night. He was thus doomed to eternal torture.

Siegfried Sassoon (1886-1967)

Educated at Marlborough and at Clare College, Cambridge. Lived in Kent and Sussex, following country pursuits especially hunting. Served in the trenches in World War I. Wounded twice and awarded the MC (which he threw away later). Organised public protest against the war.

'A VIEW OF OLD EXETER'

Pyne, a small honest painter, well content
To limn our English landscapes, worked and went,
From 1800 onward, seventy years,
Then left the world to louden in men's ears.
Here's his 'Old Exeter'; much eyed by me
Since (how time flits!) full fifteen years ago
I bought it cheap and carried it home to be
A window on my wall making me know
Old Exeter, affectionately recorded
In the now slow paced 'fifties.
                         Glancing down
From some neglected meadow near the town,
He hummed and sketched that I might be afforded
This purview of the past's provincial peace.

For J. B.Pyne Old Exeter was good;
Cows in his foreground grazed and strolled and stood:
For J. B.Pyne Victorian clumps of trees
Were golden in a bland October breeze:
Large clouds, like safe investments, loitered by;
And distant Dartmoor loomed in sombre blue,
Perpetuator of that shifting sky,
It never crossed his mind that he might do
From death such things as make me stare and sigh,—
Sigh for that afternoon he thus depicted,—
That simpler world from which we've been evicted.

Here his prim figures cruise and sit and drive
In crinolines as when they were alive.
Out of the town that man and wife are going
In smart new gig, complacently unknowing
Of their great-grandchild's air-raid-worried mind:
Into the town those gentlewomen are walking
Attuned to life, of the new Bishop talking –
Pleased that the eighteenth century's left behind,
And civically unconscious, I conjecture,
Of what it gave them in good architecture.
That group beside the cypresses adds calm
And absent-minded momentary charm
To the industrious artist's composition...
When J. B.Pyne's, this was a Devon Day.
For me it shines far far—too far—away:
For time has changed this 'View' into a Vision.

William Morris (1834-1896)

Son of a successful businessman. Educated at Marlborough and Exeter College, Oxford. Worked for an architect. Founded with Dante Gabriel Rossetti, Edward Burne-Jones and others a firm producing furniture, textiles, wallpapers, tapestry and stained glass. Lecturer, translator, poet and prose writer, he had a profound influence on political and artistic vision of his day.

from THE PROLOGUE *to* THE WANDERERS

Forget six counties overhung with smoke,
Forget the snorting steam and piston stroke,
Forget the spreading of the hideous town;
Think rather of the pack-horse on the down,
And dream of London, small, and white, and clean,
The clear Thames bordered by its gardens green...

Clive Staples Lewis (1898-1963)

Theologian, literary scholar and novelist. Studied at Oxford; became
Fellow in 1925. Appointed Chair of medieval and renaissance English
at Cambridge, 1954. Wrote science fiction trilogy with Christian mes-
sage. Became widely known for radio talks on Christianity during
World War II, and later for his seven 'Narnia' stories for children.

THE FUTURE OF FORESTRY

How will the legend of the age of trees
Feel, when the last tree falls in England?
When the concrete spreads and the town conquers
The country's heart; when contraceptive
Tarmac's laid where farm has faded,
Tramline flows where slept a hamlet,
And shop-fronts, blazing without a stop from
Dover to Wrath, have glazed us over?
Simplest tales will then bewilder
The questioning children, 'What was a chestnut?
Say what it means to climb a Beanstalk.
Tell me, grandfather, what an elm is.
What was Autumn? They never taught us.'
Then, told by teachers how once from mould
Came growing creatures of lower nature
Able to live and die, though neither
Beast nor man, and around them wreathing
Excellent clothing, breathing sunlight—
Half understanding, their ill-acquainted
Fancy will tint their wonder-paintings
—Trees as men walking, wood-romances
Of goblins stalking in silky green,
Of milk-sheen froth upon the lace of hawthorn's
Collar, pallor on the face of birchgirl.
So shall a homeless time, though dimly
Catch from afar (for soul is watchful)
A sight of tree-delighted Eden.

Robert Graves

On Dwelling

Courtesies of good-morning and good-evening
From rustic lips fail as the town encroaches:
Soon nothing passes but the cold quick stare
Of eyes that see ghosts, yet too many for fear.

Here I too walk, silent myself, in wonder
At a town not mine, though plainly coextensive
With mine, even in days coincident:
In mine I dwell, in theirs like them I haunt.

And the green country, should I turn again there?
My bumpkin neighbours loom even ghostlier:
Like trees they murmur or like blackbirds sing
Courtesies of good-morning and good-evening.

George Orwell (1903-50)

Born in Bengal. Educated at Eton. Served with Indian Imperial Police in Burma, 1922-27. Returned to work in ill-paid jobs in Paris and London. Documented post-war unemployment. Wounded fighting for the Republicans in Spanish Civil War. Famous for political satires, *Animal Farm* and *1984*.

ON A RUINED FARM NEAR THE HIS MASTERS VOICE GRAMOPHONE FACTORY

As I stand at the lichened gate
With warring worlds on either hand –
To left the black and budless trees,
The empty sties, the barns that stand

Like tumbling skeletons—and to right
The factory-towers, white and clear
Like distant, glittering cities seen
From a ship's rail—as I stand here.

I feel, and with a sharper pang,
My mortal sickness; how I give
My heart to weak and stuffless ghosts,
And with the living cannot live.

The acid smoke has soured the fields,
And browned the few and windworn flowers;
But there, where steel and concrete soar
In dizzy, geometric towers—

There, where the tapering cranes sweep round,
And great wheels turn, and trains roar by
Like strong, low-headed brutes of steel—
There is my world, my home; yet why

So alien still? For I can neither
Dwell in that world, nor turn again
To scythe and spade, but only loiter
Among the trees the smoke has slain.

Yet when the trees were young, men still
Could choose their path—the winged soul,
Not cursed with double doubts, could fly
Arrow-like to a foreseen goal;

And they who planned those soaring towers,
They too have set their spirit free;
To them their glittering world can bring
Faith, and accepted destiny;

But none to me as I stand here
Between two countries, both-ways torn,
And moveless still, like Buridan's donkey[1]
Between the water and the corn.

---

1. An ass dying of starvation through inability to choose between two equidistant and equally desirable sources of food. Specious fallacy attributed to a fourteenth century Frenchman, Jean Buridan.

John Betjeman (1906-1984)

Born in Highgate, the son of a household articles manufacturer. Educated at Marlborough and Magdalen College, Oxford. Worked briefly as a schoolmaster before beginning his career as a writer, broadcaster and journalist. Awarded a knighthood, and appointed Poet Laureate in 1972.

INEXPENSIVE PROGRESS

Encase your legs in nylons,
Bestride your hills with pylons
  O age without a soul:
Away with gentle willows
And all the elmy billows
  That through your valleys roll.

Let's say good-bye to hedges
And roads with grassy edges
  And winding country lanes;
Let all things travel faster
Where motor-car is master
  Till only Speed remains.

Destroy the ancient inn-signs
But strew the roads with tin signs
  'Keep Left,' 'M4,' 'Keep Out!'
Command, instruction, warning,
Repetitive adorning
  The rockeried roundabout;

For every raw obscenity
Must leave its small 'amenity,'
  Its patch of shaven green,
And hoardings look a wonder
In banks of floribunda
  With floodlights in between.

115

Leave no old village standing
Which could provide a landing
    For aeroplanes to roar,
But spare such cheap defacements
As huts with shattered casements
    Unlived-in since the war.

Let no provincial High Street
Which might be your or my street
    Look as it used to do,
But let the chain stores place here
Their miles of black glass facia
    And traffic thunder through.

And if there is some scenery,
Some unpretentious greenery,
    Surviving anywhere,
It does not need protecting
For soon we'll be erecting
    A Power Station there.

When all our roads are lighted
By concrete monsters sited
    Like gallows overhead,
Bathed in the yellow vomit
Each monster belches from it,
    We'll know that we are dead.

HARVEST HYMN

We spray the fields and scatter
　　The poison on the ground
So that no wicked wild flowers
　　Upon our farm be found.
We like whatever helps us
　　To line our purse with pence;
The twenty-four-hour broiler-house
　　And neat electric fence.

All concrete sheds around us
　　And Jaguars in the yard,
The telly-lounge and deep-freeze
　　Are ours from working hard.

We fire the fields for harvest,
　　The hedges swell the flame,
The oak trees and the cottages
　　From which our fathers came.
We give no compensation,
　　The earth is ours today,
And if we lose on arable,
　　Then bungalows will pay.

　　All concrete sheds....etc

Lord Dunsany

A CALL TO THE WILD

Jimson lives in a new
   Small house where the view is shrouded
With hideous hoardings, a view
   That is every year more crowded.

Every year he is vexed
   With some new noise as a neighbour;
The tramlines are coming next
   And the street is noisy with labour.

But one thing he sees afar,
   From a window over his back-door,
Is a wood as wild as a star,
   On a hill untouched by contractor.

Thither at times, forlorn,
   From the clamour of things suburban
He turns, as the Arab at dawn
   To Mecca inclines his turban.

And this is the curious prayer
   That he prays when his heart sickens,
"Oh fox come down from your lair
   And steal our chickens."

Charles Brasch (1909-73)

Editor and poet. Born of mercantile family in Dunedin, New Zealand. Educated at Waitaki High School and Oxford. Worked as an archaeologist in Egypt, then as a teacher in England. Founder in 1946 of the literary quarterly *Landfall*.

THE CITY

The walls divide us from water and from light,
Fruits are sold but do not ripen here;
We cannot tell the time of year,
And lamps and traffic estrange us from the night.

What of our fellow-citizens, the doves
And sparrows that seem now to belong here? Could
They live as freely in hedgerow and in wood
After generations of town lives?

For we have shut ourselves off from the larger world
And grown hearts narrow like alleys; we are afraid
Of quiet, emptiness, the far away.

No one knows what his neighbour is called,
But fears him; defences go up; weapons are made
To keep the unknown constantly at bay.

Wystan Hugh Auden (1907-1973)

Poet, playwright and critic. Born in York, the son of a doctor; family moved to Birmingham soon after. Educated in Surrey, Norfolk and Christ Church, Oxford. Lived briefly in Berlin, returning to work as a school teacher. Married Erika Mann to provide her with British Passport to escape Nazi Germany. Became American citizen, 1946. Professor of poetry at Oxford, 1956-60. Early writings influenced by Marx and Freud and showed strong social commitment.

from THE DOG BENEATH THE SKIN

CHORUS

The Summer holds: upon its glittering lake
Lie Europe and the islands; many rivers
Wrinkling its surface like a ploughman's palm.
Under the bellies of the grazing horses
On the far side of posts and bridges
The vigorous shadows dwindle; nothing wavers.
Calm at this moment the Dutch sea so shallow
That sunk St Pauls would ever show its golden cross
And still the deep water that divides us still from Norway.
We would show you at first an English village: You shall
     choose its location
Wherever your heart directs you most longingly to look;
     you are loving towards it:
Whether north to Scots Gap and Bellingham where the
     black rams defy the panting engine:
Or west to the Welsh Marches; to the lilting speech and
     the magicians' faces:
Wherever you were a child or had your first affair
There it stands amidst your darling scenery:
A parish bounded by the wreckers' cliff; or meadows
     where browse the Shorthorn and the maplike Frisian
As at Trent Junction where the Soar comes gliding; out
     of green Leicestershire to swell the ampler current.

120

Hiker with sunburn blisters on your office pallor,
Cross-country champion with corks in your hands,
When you have eaten your sandwich, your salt and
    your apple,
When you have begged your glass of milk from the
    ill-kept farm,
What is it you see?

I see barns falling, fences broken,
Pasture not ploughland, weeds not wheat.
The great houses remain but only half are inhabited,
Dusty the gunrooms and the stable clocks stationary.
Some have been turned into prep-schools where the diet
    is in the hands of an experienced matron,
Others into club-houses for the golf-bore and the top-hole.
Those who sang in the inns at evening have departed;
    they saw their hope in another country,
Their children have entered the service of the suburban
    areas; they have become typists, mannequins and
    factory operatives; they desired a different rhythm
    of life.
But their places are taken by another population, with
    views about nature,
Brought in charabanc and saloon along arterial roads;
Tourists to whom the Tudor cafés
Offer Bovril and buns upon Breton ware
With leather work as a sideline: Filling stations
Supplying petrol from rustic pumps.
Those who fancy themselves as foxes or desire a special
    setting for spooning
Erect their villas at the right places,
Airtight, lighted, elaborately warmed;
And nervous people who will never marry
Live upon dividends in the old-world cottages
With an animal for friend or a volume of memoirs.

Man is changed by his living; but not fast enough.
His concern to-day is for that which yesterday did not
    occur,
In the hour of the Blue Bird[1] and the Bristol Bomber,
    his thoughts are appropriate to the years of the
    Penny Farthing:
He tosses at night who at noonday found no truth...

1. Water speed record of Donald Campbell's speed-boat 'The Bluebird' on Lake Windermere.

Robert Frost

THE LINE GANG

Here come the line-gang pioneering by.
They throw a forest down less cut than broken.
They plant dead trees for living, and the dead
They string together with a living thread.
They string an instrument against the sky
Wherein words whether beaten out or spoken
Will run as hushed as when they were a thought
But in no hush they string it: they go past
With shouts afar to pull the cable taut,
To hold it hard until they make it fast,
To ease away—they have it. With a laugh,
An oath of towns that set the wild at naught
They bring the telephone and telegraph.

Spike Milligan (1918-2002)

Born in Bombay. Began writing poetry during World War II while serving with the Royal Artillery. Novelist, dramatist, actor, painter, composer, humorist, conservationist, and a founder of the radio programme, The Goon Show.

VALUES '67

Pass by citizen
    don't look left or right
Keep those drip dry eyes straight ahead.
A tree? Chop it down – it's a danger
    to lightning!
Pansies calling for water,
    Let 'em die – queer bastards –
Seek comfort in the scarlet, labour
    saving plastic rose
  Fresh with the fragrance of Daz!
Sunday! Pray citizen;
    Pray no rain will fall
    On your newly polished
    Four wheeled
    God.

    Envoi.
Beauty is in the eye of the beholder.
Get it out with Optrex.

Easter Monday 1967

Stephen Spender

The Pylons

The secret of these hills was stone, and cottages
Of that stone made,
And crumbling roads
That turned on sudden hidden villages.

Now over these small hills, they have built the concrete
That trails black wire;
Pylons, those pillars
Bare like nude giant girls that have no secret.

The valley with its gilt and evening look
And the green chestnut
Of customary root,
Are mocked dry like the parched bed of a brook.

But far above and far as sight endures
Like whips of anger
With lightning's danger
There runs the quick perspective of the future.

This dwarfs our emerald country by its trek
So tall with prophecy:
Dreaming of cities
Where often clouds shall lean their swan-white neck.

James Reeves (1909-1978)

Lecturer, critic, and editor of The Poetry Bookshelf series. Born in Middlesex. Studied English at Jesus College, Cambridge. Exempted from military service due to poor eyesight. Wrote poetry from an early age, for adults and later for children. Became virtually blind in old age.

LEAVING TOWN

It was impossible to leave the town.
Bumping across a maze of obsolete rails
Three times we reached the gasworks and reversed.
We could not get away from the canal;
Dead cats, dead hopes, in those grey deeps immersed,
Over our efforts breathed a spectral prayer.
The cattle-market and the gospel-hall
Returned like fictions of our own despair,
And like Hesperides the suburbs seemed,
Shining far off towards the guiltless fields.
We finished in a little cul-de-sac
Where on the pavement sat a ragged girl
Mourning beside a jug-and-bottle entrance.
Once more we turned the car and started back.

R. S. Thomas

AFFORESTATION

It's a population of trees
Colonising the old
Haunts of men; I prefer,
Listening to their talk,
The bare language of grass
To what the woods say,
Standing in black crowds
Under the stars at night
Or in the sun's way.
The grass feeds the sheep;
The sheep give the wool
For warm clothing, but these —?
I see the cheap times
Against which they grow:
Thin houses for dupes,
Pages of pale trash,
A world that has gone sour
With spruce. Cut them down,
They won't take the weight
Of any of the strong bodies
For which the wind sighs.

Charles Tomlinson (b.1927)

Poet, translator and artist. Born in Stoke-on-Trent. Studied at Queens'
College, Cambridge. Has taught at Bristol University since 1968. His
work as a painter is reflected in the visual qualities of his poetry.

AT STOKE

I have lived in a single landscape. Every tone
   And turn have had for their ground
These beginnings in grey-black: a land
   Too handled to be primary—all the same,
The first in feeling. I thought it once
   Too desolate, diminished and too tame
To be the foundation for anything. It straggles
   A haggard valley and lets through
Discouraged greennesses, lights from a pond or two.
   By ash-tips, or where the streets give out
In cindery in-betweens, the hills
   Swell up and free of it to where, behind
The whole vapoury, patched battlefield,
   The cows stand steaming in an acrid wind.
This place, the first to seize on my heart and eye,
   Has been their hornbook and their history.

Anthony Thwaite (b.1930)

Literary editor, lecturer and poet. Born in Chester, educated at Christ Church, Oxford. Literary career has included academic posts in Japan (1955-57) Libya (1965-67) and Kuwait (1974). Spent some years as a BBC producer and as editor of *The Listener*, *The New Statesman* and *Encounter*.

THE FORESTERS ARMS

No trees in sight except thin spindly things
Giving no shelter to animal or bird,
Not worth the pruning, valueless as fuel,
Bearing no fruit or timber: concrete acreage
Stretches about, grey packaging of soil.
On the hill-gradient no sound is heard
But lorries changing gear; no beat of wings
Of hawk or owl above this global village.
A tanker pumps in someone's Special Ale.

Scragged earth, starved grass, coke litter under rain,
Low sheds and railway sidings—factories
That ease my life with things I do not need
Dictate such stuff. And in among it all,
Its sign new-painted, chrome replacing wood,
At odds with every neighbouring thing it sees,
The Foresters Arms marks out its old domain,
Deaf to the echo of a horn's long call
And sounds of men with axes felling trees.

Douglas Dunn (b.1942)

Poet and critic. Born in Inchinnan, Renfrewshire. After reading English at Hull University worked in the library there under Philip Larkin. Returned to Scotland in 1984 and is now professor of English at St. Andrews University.

THE SILENCES

It is urban silence, it is not true silence.
The main road, growling in the distance,
Continuous, is absorbed into it;
The birds, their noises become lost in it;
Faint, civilised music decorates it.

These are edges round a quiet centre where lives are lived,
Children brought up, where television aerial fixers come,
Or priests on black bikes to lecture the tardy.
If you turn your back on it, people are only noises,
Coughs, footsteps, conversations, hands working.

They are a part of the silence of places,
The people who live here, working, falling asleep,
In a place removed one style in time outwith
The trend of places. They are like a lost tribe.
The dogs bark when strangers come, with rent books, or
    free gifts.

They move only a little from where they are fixed.
Looking at worn clothes, they sense impermanence.
They have nothing to do with where they live, the silence
    tells them.
They have looked at it so long, with such disregard,
It is baked now over their eyes like a crust.

A Removal from Terry Street

On a squeaking cart, they push the usual stuff,
A mattress, bed ends, cups, carpets, chairs,
Four paperback westerns. Two whistling youths
In surplus U.S Army battle-jackets
Remove their sister's goods. Her husband
Follows, carrying on his shoulders the son
Whose mischief we are glad to see removed,
And pushing, of all things, a lawnmower.
There is no grass in Terry Street. The worms
Come up cracks in concrete yards in moonlight.
That man, I wish him well. I wish him grass.

Horses in a Suburban Field

The road-dust settles behind the hedges
That enclose the small suburban fields.
Trees stand in straight lines, planted
By noblemen with an eye for order,
Trees in a park sold off to pay death duty.
Discarded things rot on the ground,
Paper shifts in the wind, metals rust.
Children play in the grass, like snakes,
Out of the way, on headache-soothing absences.

Sad and captured in a towny field,
The horses peep through the light,
Step over the tin cans, a bicycle frame.
They stand under a dried-up hawthorn
With dust on its leaves, smell distant kitchens.
Then they wander through the dust,
The dead dreams of housewives.

131

R. N. Allan

Born in Teeside. After working in industry and in teaching became a lecturer in French at Staffordshire University.

ELEGIES

Growing coffins,
Old grandfather Gibbon would growl,
Whenever he passed stately elms,
And the ague hard upon him.

He resented the complicity
With the skies
Of these elegant hyphens
With the earth,

But being afraid of furnaces,
Whose fiery technological worms
Betokened instant hell,

He had a secret soft spot,
For elms that were their own coffins,

Though their style seemed sure,
Furnishing town and shire with
Inevitability, fusing
With park and field a form
That had always been
Part of the definition,

Until strange beetles, *scolytus,*
Murder's absurd sponsors, came
With their doom clogs of fungus.

His full term's end
In turbulent spring,
Spared him the precocious sight
Of the dessicated limbs
Of leafless elms
Like giant stick insects
And trunks like gaunt memorials
Among the immaculate may.

His raw, undecorated stone
Stands aligned like a new recruit
Beside veterans with badges of moss
And medals of lichen.

They poke a barer sky,
Now that the elms burn
To make their own pyre.

Felling them in millions has meant
A loss of the particular that is place,
Has left a long yawn in the landscape,
And a reticence among the singing trees,
That is a dawn requiem for English elms.

Jon Bye (b.1952)

Born in Oxfordshire. Now lives in Kent, teaching in a secondary school.

Taxonomy

Towards that Definitive Catalogue
we had ridden frontiers,
taking our measure
of new worlds.

We collected specimens:
named, described, recorded.
Then in calibrated fervour
proceeded to classify.

But comprehension
failed to focus,
all lenses applied
reflecting our confusion.

So we felled, burnt clearings,
stood back to admire
and found that the forests
had vanished.

Edward Garfitt

PREDATORS

Four pies with eyes like spies,
Three jays who've seen better days,
Two daws back from the wars,
And an old crow.

No keepers now, not a gun in sight.
For the corvine tribe it's a bit of all right.
They spare no nest
Of all the rest;
Eggs they can't steal
For their morning meal
They can safely leave
To the old crow.

MAGPIE

No bird tries to kill me;
I'm not fit to feed
The chicks of lordly falcons
Or others of that breed.
The crow tribe let me be.

For I do the killing;
I who take the eggs
Of goldcrest and of pheasant.
For anything with legs,
Alive or dead, I'm willing.

I'm safe up here spying
All from east to west
As long as there's no keeper.
I see every nest
And mark things sick or dying.

They called me "chatterpie";
All folk wished me dead.
They chased rne from the village,
A price on my head.
But it's other birds that die.

Roger McGough (b.1937)

Born in Liverpool. Teacher, playwright, lecturer and writer of children's books. One of the Mersey Poets, who were active during the 1960s in reviving poetry as a public art and as entertainment. Awarded an OBE in 1997.

MOTORWAY

The politicians,
(who are buying huge cars with hobnailed wheels
   the size of merry-go-rounds)
      have a new plan.
      They are going to
      put cobbles
      in our eyesockets
      and pebbles
      in our navels
      and fill us up
      with asphalt
      and lay us
      side by side
so that we can take a more active part
      in the road
      to destruction.

Neil Astley (b.1953)

Childhood spent in Hampshire. Editor of Bloodaxe Books, which he founded in 1978 and for which he was awarded a DLitt by Newcastle University. First novel, *The End of My Tether*, is about BSE. Lives in the Tarset Valley, Northumberland.

GREAT NORTH ROAD
for Jon Silkin

Stark on the Moor's gentle slope,
sliced-off breasts
left from the motorway's great sweep
west: heaps of waste
dissembling, grassed
like knolls or barrows raised
for *eorls*. Still out,
the moon, white, crisp as frost
or cut-glass: a disk of quartz.

In sight of the city, the road's
final run thrown,
protesting, in concrete discord;
sparrows mime
on the verge (postillion
unscored, his rousing cry uttered yet unheard
as if dream dumbed him).
An old man toiling in his allotment:
the cottar[1] yoked by cornage[2] rent.

As breath condenses, he swings a spade
like clockwork, rings
the solid earth. And breaks off, eyes held
by a distant rank of trees
(French names
encountered first on maps, later

on headstones).
It's hard to make out. Each winter
they seem to retreat still further.

He orders the patch, lugging cabbage
stumps and weeds
to a compost heap sandwiched
between doors;
there adds
a fresh layer. The fork's pressure starts
the rotting process.
In three hundred million years
it's hard. Carboniferous.

1. Peasant occupying tied cottage.
2. Medieval rent based on number of beasts calculated by their horns.

Gail Bowen (b.1942)

Describes herself as 'mostly Welsh'. Lives in South London.

SUBURBAN SAVANNAH

This tidy grass
Has no right to wink
A lazy lawny eye
From the shadow at its edge,
Or to raise its back, stretch,
And alarm the lupins.

Order it to lap
Obediently at the path,
To rub around the toes
Of the big trees.
Let it be grateful for the rain,
Sit patiently and wait
For the sun to get up.

I am afraid
Once the mower fails
It will spring to the fence,
Grow yellow and ragged
And roar in the wind.

Pete Morgan (b.1939)

Poet, playwright, and writer for television. 'A Lancastrian by birth and Yorkshireman by adoption.' Served as an Infantry platoon commander in West Germany; became a pacifist in 1964 and resigned his commission. Moved to Edinburgh, then to Robin Hood's Bay, a fishing village in North Yorkshire. Now lives near York with wife, Kate.

OIL

With our eyes closed, our mouths open –
And our ears stuffed against the storm –
We slept secure enough;
Not knowing what God was sending.

To-day each wave is fringed
With the blue metallic sheen of oil.
Each strand of kelp bleeds blue
Back to the sea
And the footprints of the herring gull
Are edged in red and indigo.
On every pool and a thin skin of blue and yellow
Mirrors a quicksilver sky.

At Boggle Hole
God has been spitting oil.
Thick brown gobs of it
That smell like polish slick the rocks,
discolour sand.

The tide's reach is a trail of death –
Of feather, fin and vertebrae.
The starfish lies, contused and broken,
in smithereens of crab and claw.

There was a time

We would have named this Devil's work
For coming in October; His month
When the brambling stopped
For the club
He laid across that shrub,
The mawk he set inside the fruit.

The Devil no longer holds good. He
Was all in evil then
As God sat favoured in his sky –
Worshipped. feated, all-seeing.

As one has dropped from favour
So's the other.
We now dismiss the Devil's work. -
Set all of that behind us.

An oil slick on the shore's
An act of God
And the next tide takes away his dead.

Bernard Saint (b.1950)

Born in Cheshire. First poems published in magazines and anthologies in his mid-teens. Influenced by the American 'beat' poets. Has worked for two decades as a group therapist, working in adult psychiatry and in the treatment of substance abuse.

'WHAT I AM'

What I am
a white chalk man between chalk walls.

Where is the pulse that linked my blood to flowers?
Where, my white children?
Pale from your cold beds of pale sheets I see
you have lost the lusty
copra sinew, the hard copper jaw
the rhythm in your stiffened loins has lost its ecstasy.

Sad man with befloured face and buttered hair
your smeared grin mocks the gentle alchemy of Nature
You desecrate the hillside with pylons,
the body with clothes
What right have you to bring flowers
to the graves of your blossoming dead?

I will walk your metallic hills no more
Nor tread your asphalt plains.
I would hear the forgotten drums echo out
from lost savannahs,
remember the noonday heat on a naked thigh.

When I hear the rhythm in the wings of cranes
or the highproud jazz of Parker or Coltrane
rear up above rooftops
The pallor of my soul turns into shadow

My blood like molten bronze pounds deep in my chalk skull
the dark poetry of the basic man
moulds my molten thoughts.

In your church services
The tense atmosphere of the musty air
reminds me of the voodoo rite before the drums begin.
Crow of Cock! Blood of Goat! and the drumming
of bare feet on sand

I am sacrificed in these harsh steel corridors
to the white man's god
of cities and despair.

PART FOUR

SPIRIT OF PLACE

St. Augustine of Hippo (354-430 AD)

Born near Tunis, son of a pagan father and a Christian mother. Great scholar, lectured in philosophy. Became Bishop of Hippo in Roman Africa, and the founder of a religious order. Resolute fighter for his faith, wrote *The City of God* and the *Confessions*, which tells the story of his early career.

from THE CONFESSIONS

...and men go forth, and admire lofty mountains and broad seas, and roaring torrents, and the ocean, and the course of stars, and forget themselves...

John Clare

I AM

I am—yet what I am, none cares or knows;
  My friends forsake me like a memory lost:
I am the self-consumer of my woes—
  They rise and vanish in oblivions host,
Like shadows in love frenzied stifled throes
  And yet I am, and live—like vapours tossed

Into the nothingness of scorn and noise,
  Into the living sea of waking dreams,
Where there is neither sense of life or joys,
  But the vast shipwreck of my lifes esteems;
Even the dearest that I love the best
  Are strange—nay, rather, stranger than the rest.

I long for scenes where man hath never trod
  A place where woman never smiled or wept
There to abide with my Creator God,
  And sleep as I in childhood sweetly slept,
Untroubling and untroubled where I lie
  The grass below, above, the vaulted sky.

George Gordon Byron, 6th Lord
(1788–1824)

Born in London. Son of Captain 'Mad Jack' Byron, who died when Byron was three, and Catherine Gordon, a Scottish heiress descended from James I of Scotland. Childhood spent in Aberdeenshire. Inherited Newstead Abbey at the age of 10. Educated at Harrow and Cambridge where he published first poems. Toured the Mediterranean. Had love affair with Lady Caroline Lamb. Married Annabella Milbanke in 1815. Marriage lasted for about a year. Left England in 1816 and never returned. Fired with determination to free Greece from Turks, formed The Byron Brigade, but died of fever in Missolonghi before action began.

from CHILDE HAROLD'S PILGRIMAGE
(CANTO IV)

> There is a pleasure in the pathless woods,
> There is a rapture on the lonely shore,
> There is society, where none intrudes,
> By the deep Sea, and music in its roar:
> I love not Man the less, but Nature more,
> From these our interviews, in which I steal
> From all I may be, or have been before,
> To mingle with the Universe, and feel
> What I can ne'er express, yet can not all conceal.

Robert Bridges (1844-1930)

Born in Kent. Educated at Eton and Corpus Christi, Oxford. Studied medicine at Bartholomews Hospital. Poet, playwright, essayist and critic; interested in the musical setting of poetry. Appointed Poet Laureate in 1913.

NIGHTINGALES

Beautiful must be the mountains whence ye come,
And bright in the fruitful valleys the streams, wherefrom
　　　　Ye learn your song:
Where are those starry woods? O might I wander there,
　　Among the flowers, which in that heavenly air
　　　　Bloom the year long!

Nay, barren are those mountains and spent the streams:
Our song is the voice of desire, that haunts our dreams,
　　　　A throe of the heart,
Whose pining visions dim, forbidden hopes profound,
　　No dying cadence nor long sigh can sound,
　　　　For all our art.

Alone, aloud in the raptured ear of men
We pour our dark nocturnal secret; and then,
　　　　As night is withdrawn
From these sweet-springing meads and bursting boughs of May,
　　Dream, while the innumerable choir of day
　　　　Welcome the dawn.

150

W. B. Yeats

THE LAKE ISLE OF INNISFREE

I will arise and go now, and go to Innisfree,
And a small cabin build there, of clay and wattles made:
Nine bean-rows will I have there, a hive for the honey-bee,
And live alone in the bee-loud glade.

And I shall have some peace there, for peace comes dropping slow,
Dropping from the veils of the morning to where the cricket sings;
There midnight's all a glimmer, and noon a purple glow,
And evening full of the linnet's wings.

I will arise and go now, for always night and day
I hear lake water lapping with low sounds by the shore;
While I stand on the roadway, or on the pavements grey,
I hear it in the deep heart's core.

Rudyard Kipling (1865-1936)

Poet, short-story writer and novelist. Born in Bombay, the son of an art teacher. After schooling in England returned to India and began career as a journalist. Early poems and stories were published in booklets published by the Indian Railway Library and in newspapers. In 1907 became the first English writer to receive the Nobel Prize for literature.

THE WAY THROUGH THE WOODS

They shut the road through the woods
Seventy years ago.
Weather and rain have undone it again,
And now you would never know
There was once a road through the woods
Before they planted the trees.
It is underneath the coppice and heath
And the thin anemones.
Only the keeper sees
That, where the ring-dove broods,
And the badgers roll at ease,
There was once a road through the woods.

Yet, if you enter the woods
Of a summer evening late,
When the night-air cools on the trout-ringed pools
Where the otter whistles his mate,
(They fear not men in the woods,
Because they see so few.)
You will hear the beat of a horse's feet,
And the swish of a skirt in the dew,
Steadily cantering through
The misty solitudes,
As though they perfectly knew
The old lost road through the woods...
But there is no road through the woods.

William Wordsworth

from THE PRELUDE
*(*BOOK I. CHILDHOOD AND SCHOOLTIME*)*

  One summer evening (led by her) I found
A little boat tied to a willow tree
Within a rocky cave, its usual home.
Straight I unloosed her chain, and stepping in
Pushed from the shore. It was an act of stealth
And troubled pleasure, nor without the voice
Of mountain echoes did my boat move on;
Leaving behind her still, on either side,
Small circles glittering idly in the moon,
Until they melted all into one track
Of sparkling light. But now, like one who rows,
Proud of his skill, to reach a chosen point
With an unswerving line, I fixed my view
Upon the summit of a craggy ridge,
The horizon's utmost boundary; for above
Was nothing but the stars and the grey sky.
She was an elfin pinnace; lustily
I dipped my oars into the silent lake,
And, as I rose upon the stroke, my boat
Went heaving through the water like a swan;
When, from behind that craggy steep till then
The horizon's bound, a huge peak, black and huge,
As if with voluntary power instinct,
Upreared its head. I struck and struck again,
And growing still in stature the grim shape
Towered up between me and the stars, and still,
For so it seemed, with purpose of its own
And measured motion like a living thing,
Strode after me. With trembling hands I turn'd,
And through the silent water stole my way
Back to the cavern of the willow tree.
There, in her mooring.place, I left my bark,

And through the meadows homeward went, in grave
And serious mood; but after I had seen
That spectacle, for many days, my brain
Work'd with a dim and undetermin'd sense
Of unknown modes of being; o'er my thoughts
There hung a darkness, call it solitude
Or blank desertion. No familiar shapes
remained, no pleasant images of trees,
Of sea or sky, no colours of green fields;
But huge and mighty forms, that do not live
Like living men, mov'd slowly through the mind
By day, and were a trouble to my dreams.

John Masefield (1878-1967)

Had an idyllic childhood in Ledbury, Herefordshire. Joined the merchant navy aged 13 and sailed for Chile three years later; suffered from seasickness. On second voyage deserted ship and did various jobs in America. Returned to England to work on *The Manchester Guardian*; a prolific writing career followed. Appointed Poet Laureate in 1930. Received the Order of Merit in 1935.

'UP ON THE DOWNS'

Up on the downs the red-eyed kestrels hover,
Eyeing the grass.
The field-mouse flits like a shadow into cover
As their shadows pass.

Men are burning the gorse on the down's shoulder;
A drift of smoke
Glitters with fire and hangs, and the skies smoulder,
And the lungs choke.

Once the tribe did thus on the downs, on these downs burning
Men in the frame,
Crying to the gods of the downs till their brains were turning
And the gods came.

And to-day on the downs, in the wind, the hawks the grasses,
In blood and air,
Something passes me and cries as it passes,
On the chalk downland bare.

Martin Armstrong (1882-1974)

Editor and short-story writer as well as poet. Wrote the popular poem
'Miss Thompson Goes Shopping'. Edited *The Essential Mary Webb*,
first published in 1949.

GOING UP THE LINE

O consolation and refreshment breathed
From the young Spring with apple-blossom wreathed,
    Whose certain coming blesses
All life with token of immortality,
And from the ripe beauty and human tendernesses
And reconcilement and tranquillity
Which are the spirit of all things grown old.
    For now that I have seen
The curd-white hawthorn once again
    Break out on the new green,
And through the iron gates in the long blank wall
    Have viewed across a screen
Of rosy apple-blossom the grey spire
And low red roofs and humble chimney-stacks,
And stood in spacious courtyards of old farms,
And heard green virgin wheat sing to the breeze,
And the drone of ancient worship rise and fall
In the dark church, and talked with simple folk
Of farm and village, dwelling near the earth,
Among earth's ancient elemental things:
    I can with heart made bold
Go back into the ways of ruin and death
With step unflagging and with quiet breath,
For drawn from the hidden Spirit's deepest well
I carry in my soul a power to quell
    All ills and terrors such as these can hold.

156

Siegfried Sassoon

THE HAWTHORN TREE

Not much to me is yonder lane
   Where I go every day;
But when there's been a shower of rain
   And hedge-birds whistle gay,
I know my lad that's out in France
   With fearsome things to see
Would give his eyes for just one glance
   At our white hawthorn tree.

Not much to me is yonder lane
   Where *he* so longs to tread:
But when there's been a shower of rain
I think I'll never weep again
   Until I've heard he's dead.

BREAK OF DAY

There seemed a smell of autumn in the air
At the bleak end of night; he shivered there
In a dank, musty dug-out where he lay,
Legs wrapped in sand-bags,—lumps of chalk and clay
Spattering his face. Dry-mouthed, he thought, 'To-day
We start the damned attack; and, Lord knows why,
Zero's at nine; how bloody if I'm done in
Under the freedom of that morning sky!'
And then he coughed and dozed, cursing the din.

Was it the ghost of autumn in that smell
Of underground, or God's blank heart grown kind,
That sent a happy dream to him in hell?—
Where men are crushed like clods, and crawl to find
Some crater for their wretchedness; who lie
In outcast immolation, doomed to die

157

Far from clean things or any hope of cheer,
Cowed anger in their eyes, till darkness brims
And roars into their heads, and they can hear
Old childish talk, and tags of foolish hymns.

He sniffs the chilly air; (his dreaming starts),
He's riding in a dusty Sussex lane
In quiet September; slowly night departs;
And he's a living soul, absolved from pain.
Beyond the brambled fences where he goes
Are glimmering fields with harvest piled in sheaves,
And tree-tops dark against the stars grown pale;
Then, clear and shrill, a distant farm-cock crows;
And there's a wall of mist along the vale
Where willows shake their watery-sounding leaves,
He gazes on it all, and scarce believes
That earth is telling its old peaceful tale;
He thanks the blessed world that he was born...
Then, far away, a lonely note of the horn.

They're drawing the Big Wood! Unlatch the gate,
And set Golumpus going on the grass;
He knows the corner where it's best to wait
And hear the crashing woodland chorus pass;
The corner where old foxes make their track
To the Long Spinney; that's the place to be.
The bracken shakes below an ivied tree,
And then a cub looks out; and 'Tally-o-back!'
He bawls, and swings his thong with volleying crack,—
All the clean thrill of autumn in his blood,
And hunting surging through him like a flood
In joyous welcome from the untroubled past;
While the war drifts away, forgotten at last.

Now a red, sleepy sun above the rim
Of twilight stares along the quiet weald,
And the kind, simple country shines revealed

In solitudes of peace, no longer dim.
The old horse lifts his face and thanks the light,
Then stretches down his head to crop the green.
All things that he has loved are in his sight;
The places where his happiness has been
Are in his eyes, his heart, and they are good.

      .   .   .   .

Hark! there's the horn: they're drawing the Big Wood.

DECEMBER STILLNESS

December stillness, teach me through your trees
That loom along the west, one with the land,
The veiled evangel of your mysteries.
    While nightfall, sad and spacious, on the down
    Deepens, and dusk imbues me, where I stand,
    With grave diminishings of green and brown,
    Speak, roofless Nature, your instinctive words;
    And let me learn your secret from the sky,
    Following a flock of steadfast-journeying birds
    In lone remote migration beating by.
December stillness, crossed by twilight roads,
Teach me to travel far and bear my loads.

Vita Sackville-West (1892-1962)

Poet, novelist, biographer; born in Kent. Married Harold Nicholson, travelling with him in his diplomatic career. Settled at Sissinghurst, Kent, devoting much time to her garden. Close friend of Virginia Woolf.

from THE LAND — WINTER

I sing the cycle of my country's year,
I sing the tillage, and the reaping sing,
Classic monotony, that modes and wars
Leave undisturbed, unbettered, for their best
Was born immediate, of expediency.
The sickle sought no art; the axe, the share
Draped no superfluous beauty round their steel;
The scythe desired no music for her stroke,
Her stroke sufficed in music, as her blade
Laid low the swathes; the scythesmen swept, nor cared
What crop had ripened, whether oats in Greece
Or oats in Kent; the shepherd on the ridge
Like his Boeotian forebear kept his flocks,
And still their outlines on our tenderer sky
Simple and classic rear their grave design
As once at Thebes, as once in Lombardy.

I sing once more
The mild continuous epic of the soil,
Haysel and harvest, tilth and husbandry;
I tell of marl and dung, and of the means
That break the unkindly spirit of the clay;
I tell the things I know, the things I knew
Before I knew them, immemorially…

from THE LAND — WINTER

The country habit has me by the heart,
For he's bewitched forever who has seen,
Not with his eyes but with his vision, Spring
Flow down the woods and stipple leaves with sun,
As each man knows the life that fits him best,
The shape it makes in his soul, the tune, the tone,
And after ranging on a tentative flight
Stoops like the merlin to the constant lure.
The country habit has me by the heart.
I never hear the sheep-bells in the fold,
Nor see the ungainly heron rise and flap
Over the marsh, nor hear the asprous corn
Clash, as the reapers set the sheaves in shocks
(That like a tented army dream away
The night beneath the moon in silver fields),
Nor watch the stubborn team of horse and man
Graven upon the skyline, nor regain
The sign-posts on the roads towards my home
Bearing familiar names—without a strong
Leaping of recognition; only here
Lies peace after uneasy truancy;
Here meet and marry many harmonies,
—All harmonies being ultimately one,—
Small mirroring majestic; for as earth
Rolls on her journey, so her little fields
Ripen or sleep, and the necessities
Of seasons match the planetary law.

William Wordsworth

from THE PRELUDE
(BOOK I. CHILDHOOD AND SCHOOLTIME)

Wisdom and Spirit of the universe!
Thou Soul that art the eternity of thought!
That givest to forms and images a breath
And everlasting motion! not in vain,
By day or star-light thus from my first dawn
Of Childhood didst Thou intertwine for me
The passions that build up our human Soul,
Not with the mean and vulgar works of Man,
But with high objects, with enduring things,
With life and nature, purifying thus
The elements of feeling and of thought,
And sanctifying, by such discipline,
Both pain and fear, until we recognise
A grandeur in the beatings of the heart.

Nor was this fellowship vouchsafed to me
With stinted kindness. In November days,
When vapours, rolling down the valleys, made
A lonely scene more lonesome; among woods
At noon, and 'mid the calm of summer nights,
When, by the margin of the trembling Lake,
Beneath the gloomy hills, homeward I went
In solitude, such intercourse was mine;
'Twas mine among the fields both day and night,
And by the waters all the summer long.

And in the frosty season, when the sun
Was set, and, visible for many a mile,
The cottage windows through the twilight blazed,
I heeded not the summons: – happy time

It was, indeed, for all of us; to me
It was a time of rapture! Clear and loud
The village-clock tolled six; I wheeled about,
Proud and exulting, like an untired horse,
That cares not for his home. – All shod with steel,
We hissed along the polished ice, in games
Confederate, imitative of the chase
And woodland pleasures – the resounding horn,
The pack loud chiming, and the hunted hare.
So through the darkness and the cold we flew,
And not a voice was idle; with the din
Smitten, the precipices rang aloud;
The leafless trees and every icy crag
Tinkled like iron; while far-distant hills
Into the tumult sent an alien sound
Of melancholy not unnoticed, while the stars,
Eastward, were sparkling clear, and in the west
The orange sky of evening died away.

Ezra Pound (1885-1975)

American poet of Quaker ancestry, born in Idaho. Sailed for Europe in 1908, went to live in Venice. Married Dorothy in 1914, moved to Paris in 1920 and Italy in 1924. Became anti-semitic and pro Mussolini. Arrested for broadcasting propaganda in 1945. Sent to American disciplinary centre at Pisa, then transferred to the USA where he was declared insane and confined to a hospital. Released in 1958 and returned to die in Italy.

THE TREE

I stood still and was a tree amid the wood,
Knowing the truth of things unseen before;
Of Daphne and the laurel bow[1]
And that god-feasting couple old
That grew elm-oak amid the wold.
'Twas not until the gods had been
Kindly entreated, and been brought within
Unto the hearth of their heart's home
That they might do this wonder thing;
Nathless I have been a tree amid the wood
And many a new thing understood
That was rank folly to my head before.

1. Daughter of the River God Peneus; pursued by Apollo, she is turned into a laurel tree by Mother Earth, just as Apollo is about to reach her.

Cecil Day-Lewis

THE GATE

In the foreground, clots of cream-white flowers (meadow-sweet?
Guelder? Cow parsley?): a patch of green: then a gate
Dividing the green from a brown field: and beyond,
By steps of mustard and sainfoin-pink, the distance
Climbs right-handed away
Up to an olive hilltop and the sky.

The gate it is, dead-centre, ghost-amethyst-hued,
Fastens the whole together like a brooch.
It is all arranged, all there, for the gate's sake
Or for what may come through the gate. But those white flowers,
Craning their necks, putting their heads together,
Like a crowd that holds itself back from surging forward,
Have their own point of balance – poised, it seems,
On the airy brink of whatever it is they await.

And I, gazing over their heads from outside the picture,
Question what we are waiting for: not summer –
Summer is here in charlock, grass and sainfoin.
A human event? – but there's no path to the gate,
Nor does it look as if it was meant to open.
The ghost of one who often came this way
When there was a path? I do not know. But I think,
If I could go deep into the heart of the picture

From the flowers' point of view, all I would ask is
Not that the gate should open, but that it should
Stay there, holding the coloured folds together.
We expect nothing (the flowers might add), we only
Await: this pure awaiting –
It is the kind of worship we are taught.

165

R. S. Thomas

THE MOOR

It was like a church to me.
I entered it on soft foot,
Breath held like a cap in the hand.
It was quiet.
What God was there made himself felt,
Not listened to, in clean colours
That brought a moistening of the eye,
In movement of the wind over grass.

There were no prayers said. But stillness
Of the heart's passions—that was praise
Enough; and the mind's cession
Of its kingdom. I walked on,
Simple and poor, while the air crumbled
And broke on me generously as bread.

W. B. Yeats

In the Seven Woods

I have heard the pigeons of the Seven Woods[1]
Make their faint thunder, and the garden bees
Hum in the lime-tree flowers; and put away
The unavailing outcries and the old bitterness
That empty the heart. I have forgot awhile
Tara uprooted[2], and new commonness[3]
Upon the throne and crying about the streets
And hanging its paper flowers[4] from post to post,
Because it is alone of all things happy.
I am contented, for I know that Quiet
Wanders laughing and eating her wild heart
Among pigeons and bees, while that Great Archer[5],
Who but awaits His hour to shoot, still hangs
A cloudy quiver over Pairc-na-lee.[6]

1. Part of Coole Park Estate owned by Yeat's close friend Lady Gregory.
2. Prehistoric burial site and seat of ancient Irish Kings. 'Uprooted' because of recent excavations.
3. Edward VII, Queen Victoria's dissolute son.
4. Edward VII's Coronation decorations in Dublin.
5. The Constellation, Sagittarius.
6. 'The field of the calves' – one of the seven woods.

Thomas Stearns Eliot (1888-1965)

Poet, playwright and critic. Born in St. Louis, Missouri. Educated at Harvard, the Sorbonne and Oxford. Married Vivien Haigh-Wood in 1915, settled in London. Taught and reviewed books; then worked for Lloyds Bank, 1917-1925. *The Waste Land*, published in 1922, established his reputation. Became a British citizen in 1927. Awarded the Nobel Prize for literature in 1948, and the Order of Merit the same year.

from FOUR QUARTETS
(THE DRY SALVAGES)

I do not know much about gods; but I think that the river
Is a strong brown god – sullen, untamed and intractable,
Patient to some degree, at first recognised as a frontier;
Useful, untrustworthy, as a conveyor of commerce;
Then only a problem confronting the builder of bridges.
The problem once solved, the brown god is almost forgotten
By the dwellers in cities – ever, however, implacable,
Keeping his seasons and rages, destroyer, reminder
Of what men choose to forget. Unhonoured, unpropitiated
By worshippers of the machine, but waiting, watching and
        waiting.
His rhythm was present in the nursery bedroom,
In the rank ailanthus of the April dooryard,
In the smell of grapes on the autumn table,
And the evening circle in the winter gaslight.

  The river is within us, the sea is all about us;
The sea is the land's edge also, the granite
Into which it reaches, the beaches where it tosses
Its hints of earlier and other creation:
The starfish, the horseshoe crab, the whale's backbone;
The pools where it offers to our curiosity
The more delicate algae and the sea anemone.
It tosses up our losses, the torn seine,

168

The shattered lobsterpot, the broken oar
And the gear of foreign dead men. The sea has many voices,
Many gods and many voices.

                          The salt is on the briar rose,
The fog is in the fir trees.

Mervyn Peake (1911-1968)

Novelist, poet and artist. Born in Kuling, China, the son of a medical missionary. Moved to Kent aged 11, later studied at the Royal Academy. Worked as an artist on the isle of Sark for three years. Returned to London, taught art, and published verse and stories for children. Invalided out of army in 1943 after nervous breakdown. Commissioned as war artist; visited Belsen in 1945. His last years were overshadowed by Parkinson's disease.

WITH PEOPLE, SO WITH TREES

With people, so with trees: where there are groups
Of either, men or trees, some will remain
Aloof while others cluster where one stoops
To breathe some dusky secret. Some complain

And some gesticulate and some are blind;
Some toss their heads above green towns; some freeze
For lack of love in copses of mankind;
Some laugh; some mourn; with people, so with trees.

Patricia Beer (b.1924)

Born in Devon, the daughter of a railway clerk and a Plymouth Brethren mother. Worked as an English lecturer in Italy and at Goldsmith's, London. The legends and landscapes of the West Country form the background for many of her poems.

SUMMER SONG FOR ME AND MY AUNTS

Never forget the moors
Behind the house, never
Let being a woman
Or the baking of bread
Or sizing up a sermon

Keep you off the heath
And far from the stone wall
That is no more than gauze
To these strong winds.
Headaches come indoors.

Walk uphill from the house
And the graves already there.
The chill of waterfalls
Cannot cause worse coughing
Than sprig-papered walls

Where you die in turn
On a narrow sofa
Boxed up from the storm.
Dying women can walk
On the moors without harm.

Charles Tomlinson

FOXES' MOON

Night over England's interrupted pastoral,
  And moonlight on the frigid lattices
Of pylons. The shapes of dusk
  Take on an edge, refined
By a drying wind and foxes bring
  Flint hearts and sharpened senses to
This desolation of grisaille in which the dew
  Grows clearer, colder. Foxes go
In their ravenous quiet to where
  The last farm meets the first
Row from the approaching town: they nose
  The garbage of the yards, move through
The white displacement of a daily view
  Uninterrupted. Warm sleepers turn,
Catch the thin volpine bark between
  Dream on dream, then lose it
To the babbling undertow they swim. These
  Are the fox hours, cleansed
Of all the meanings we can use
  And so refuse them. Foxes glow,
Ghosts unacknowledged in the moonlight
  Of the suburb, and like ghosts they flow
Back, racing the coming red, the beams
  Of early cars, a world not theirs
Gleaming from kindled windows, asphalt, wires.

James Reeves

BESIDE THE RIVER

I know that silver trees beside the river
When first light thins a milk-and-water mist
Cannot be otherwise than calm and helpless
– A maiden grove.

Then why should such a picture disconcert me,
Flooding the mind with purposeless regret,
As if those leaves were Daphne's hair transformed[1]
And I Apollo?

1. Daughter of the River God Peneus; pursued by Apollo, she is turned into a laurel tree by Mother Earth, just as Apollo is about to reach her. Her hair turns into the leaves first.

Ted Hughes

A WIND FLASHES THE GRASS

Leaves pour blackly across.
We cling to the earth, with glistening eyes, pierced afresh
                                by the tree's cry.

And the incomprehensible cry
From the boughs, in the wind
Sets us listening for below words,
Meanings that will not part from the rock.

The trees thunder in unison, on a gloomy afternoon,
And the ploughman grows anxious, his tractor becomes
    terrible,
As his memory litters downwind
And the shadow of his bones tosses darkly on the air.

The trees suddenly storm to a stop in a hush
Against the sky, where the field ends.
And crowd there shuddering
And wary, like horses bewildered by lightning.

The stirring of their twigs against the dark, travelling sky
Is the oracle of the earth

They too are afraid they too are momentary
Streams rivers of shadow.

Margaret Buckle

THE MOORLAND ROAD

There is nobody here.
The road runs over the moor.
The bare hills fold round it.
The sun streams down on it.
The wind moves over it.
There is nobody here.
The harsh grass hisses.
The beck purls and chuckles over the stones.
With a whirr and a thrumming,
A bird stoops from the hill.
Silence is made up of many voices.
I am thirsty for silence.
It soaks into my dryness like rainwater.
My dusty thoughts grow green again.
I could grow here for a hundred years.

Cottout
Rannock Moor

Laurie Lee

INVASION SUMMER

The evening, the heather,
the unsecretive cuckoo
and butterflies in their disorder,
not a word of war as we lie
our mouths in a hot nest
and the flowers advancing.

Does a hill defend itself,
does a river run to earth
to hide its quaint neutrality?
A boy is shot with England in his brain,
but she lies brazen yet beneath the sun,
she has no honour and she has no fear.

HOME FROM ABROAD

Far-fetched with tales of other worlds and ways,
My skin well-oiled with wines of the Levant,
I set my face into a filial smile
To greet the pale, domestic kiss of Kent.

But shall I never learn? That gawky girl,
Recalled so primly in my foreign thoughts,
Becomes again the green-haired queen of love
Whose wanton form dilates as it delights.

Her rolling tidal landscape floods the eye
And drowns Chianti in a dusky stream;
The flower-flecked grasses swim with simple horses
The hedges choke with roses fat as cream.

So do I breathe the hayblown airs of home,
And watch the sea-green elms drip birds and shadows,
And as the twilight nets the plunging sun
My heart's keel slides to rest among the meadows.

Brian Patten (b.1946)

Born in Liverpool. One of the Mersey poets. Began writing career on the *Bootle Times*. Worked as a lecturer in San Diego. Poet, playwright, and writer of children's books.

FROGS IN THE WOOD

How good it would be to be lost again,
Night falling on the compass and the map
Turning to improbable flames,
Bright ashes going out in the ponds.

And how good it would be
To stand bewildered in a strange wood
Where you are the loudest thing,
Your heart making a deafening noise.

And how strange when your fear of being lost has subsided
To stand listening to the frogs holding
Their arguments in the streams,
Condemning the barbarous herons.

And how right it is
To shrug off real and invented grief
As of no importance
To this moment of your life,

When being lost seems
So much more like being found,
And you find all that is lost
Is what weighed you down.

Bert Ward (b.1922)

Born in North Ormesby, Middlesborough, the son of shipyard worker. Served in Royal Navy during World War II. After years of unskilled and semi-skilled work, went to Ruskin College on a trade union scholarship, and then to the London School of Economics as a mature student. Joined the Communist Party, 1948. Worked as a lecturer in South-East London College for twenty years. Helped create a cross-party peace proup in Ireland; currently editing its bulletin *New Dialogue*.

AND SEND THE TIME AWAY

Cowslip, harebell, meadow rue,
The hedges white with may,
I touch your hair
And kiss your cheek,
And send the time away.

Shepherd's purse and saxifrage,
Columbine, caraway,
I take you gently in my arms,
And send the time away.

Snow goose skies,
And bleak hedgerows
At dusking of the day,
You hold my head close to your breast
And send the time away.

Brian Patten

A Talk with a Wood

Moving through you one evening
when you offered shelter to
quiet things soaked in rain

I saw through your thinning branches
the beginnings of suburbs, and
frightened by the rain,

gray hares running upright in
distant fields, and quite alone there
thought of nothing but my footprints

being filled, and love, distilled
of people, drifted free, and then
the woods spoke with me.

William Wordsworth

LINES COMPOSED A FEW MILES ABOVE TINTERN ABBEY...
JULY 13, 1798

.....................And so I dare to hope,
Though changed, no doubt, from what I was when first
I came among these hills; when like a roe
I bounded o'er the mountains, by the sides
Of the deep rivers, and the lonely streams,
Wherever nature led: more like a man
Flying from something that he dreads, than one
Who sought the thing he loved. For nature then
(The coarser pleasures of my boyish days,
And their glad animal movements all gone by)
To me was all in all.—I cannot paint
What then I was. The sounding cataract
Haunted me like a passion: the tall rock,
The mountain, and the deep and gloomy wood,
Their colours and their forms, were then to me
An appetite; a feeling and a love,
That had no need of a remoter charm,
By thought supplied, nor any interest
Unborrowed from the eye.—That time is past,
And all its aching joys are now no more,
And all its dizzy raptures. Not for this
Faint I, nor mourn nor murmur; other gifts
Have followed; for such loss, I would believe,
Abundant recompence. For I have learned
To look on nature, not as in the hour
Of thoughtless youth; but hearing oftentimes
The still, sad music of humanity,
Nor harsh nor grating, though of ample power
To chasten and subdue. And I have felt
A presence that disturbs me with the joy
Of elevated thoughts; a sense sublime
Of something far more deeply interfused,

180

Whose dwelling is the light of setting suns,
And the round ocean and the living air,
And the blue sky, and in the mind of man;
A motion and a spirit, that impels
All thinking things, all objects of all thought,
And rolls through all things...

Rudyard Kipling

'CITIES AND THRONES AND POWERS'

Cities and Thrones and Powers
  Stand in Time's eye,
Almost as long as flowers,
  Which daily die:
But, as new buds put forth
  To glad new men,
Out of the spent and unconsidered Earth
  The Cities rise again.

This season's Daffodil,
  She never hears
What change, what chance, what chill,
  Cut down last year's;
But with bold countenance,
  And knowledge small,
Esteems her seven days' continuance
  To be perpetual.

So Time that is o'er-kind
  To all that be,
Ordains us e'en as blind,
  As bold as she:
That in our very death,
  And burial sure,
Shadow to shadow, well persuaded, saith,
  'See how our works endure!'

Laurence Binyon (1869-1943)

Poet, art historian and critic. Born in Lancaster. Became keeper of the Department of Oriental Prints and Books in the British Museum, where he worked for forty years, becoming an authority on Oriental art. His poems include the famous war elegy, 'For the Fallen' ('They shall not grow old, as we that are left grow old…').

THE BURNING OF THE LEAVES

Now is the time for the burning of the leaves.
They go to the fire; the nostril pricks with smoke
Wandering slowly into a weeping mist.
Brittle and blotched, ragged and rotten sheaves!
A flame siezes the smouldering ruin and bites
On stubborn stalks that crackle as they resist.

The last hollyhock's fallen tower is dust;
All the spices of June are a bitter reek,
All the extravagant riches spent and mean.
All burns! The reddest rose is a ghost;
Sparks whirl up, to expire in the mist: the wild
Fingers of fire are making corruption clean.

Now is the time for stripping the spirit bare,
Time for the burning of days ended and done.
Idle solace of things that have gone before:
Rootless hope and fruitless desire are there;
Let them go to the fire, with never a look behind.
The world that was ours is a world that is ours no more.

They will come again, the leaf and the flower, to arise
From squalor of rottenness into the old splendour,
And magical scents to a wondering memory bring;
The same glory, to shine upon different eyes.
Earth cares for her own ruins, naught for ours.
Nothing is certain, only the certain spring.

Robert Rendall

KIRKYARD BY THE SHORE

In this old kirkyard lay my coffined bones,
That I, perchance, like those within these graves,
On winter nights may hear the waves
Thundering among the stones

Anon (Early 13th Century)

Pity for Mary[1]

Now goth sonne under wod[2]:
Me reweth, Marye, thy faire rode.[3]
Now goth sonne under Tre:
Me reweth, Marye, thy sone and thee.

1. The poet has a vision of Christ on the cross as the sun goes down.
2. Wood (of the cross)
3. I feel pity, Mary, for your fair face.

Index of First Lines

INDEX OF AUTHORS

191

193

Acknowledgements

Firstly I want to thank the Director of the A.R.C. Addington Fund, Ian Bell and his Deputy Director, Sue Eeley for their wonderful support and enthusiasm. Secondly, Oliver Campbell for typing the manuscript. I am indebted to Sir Nicholas Harington and John Lamb for their advice; to the Hon. Seymour Fortescue for his time and imagination in steadying my nerve to raise the production costs; to the staff of the Poetry Library in the Royal Festival Hall; to my dear friends Professor Robin Grove White and Clifford Simmons. A very special thank you to Kemal Akthar for his constant technical assistance. I also wish to thank Diana Dunwoodie for her steady encouragement when my confidence was waning. Lastly, I would like to acknowledge the contribution of Merlin Unwin and Anthony Bloor who gave their time and expertise as a gift to the Rank Foundation Fund. Without their help this anthology would never have seen the light of day.

Permission to use copyright material is gratefullly acknowledged to the following:

R. Dardis Clarke for 'The Fair at Windgap' from *Collected Poems* by Austin Clarke (published by Dolmen Press in association with Oxford University Press).

The Orion Publishing Group Ltd for 'The Moor', 'Afforestation' and 'On the Farm' from *Collected Poems* by R.S. Thomas (published by J.M Dent).

Anvil Press Poetry Ltd for 'Berkshire's Ancient Man' from *Collected Poems* 1941-1994 by Michael Hamburger.

John Murray (Publishers) Ltd for 'Roads' from *Collected Poems* by George Mackay Brown; 'Inexpensive Progress' from *Collected Poems 1956* by John Betjeman; and 'Harvest Hymn' from *Collected Poems 1958* by John Betjeman.

Paul Coltman for 'Old Bird Names' and 'Pulborough Old Bridge'.

Envoi magazine for 'Muckspreading' by Geoffrey K. Nelson.

R.P. Rendall for two poems by his uncle, Robert Rendall,

from *Country Sonnets and Other Poems* (published by The Kirkwell Press).

PFD for 'Day of These Days', 'Invasion Summer' and 'Home from Abroad' by Laurie Lee; 'The Gate' and 'Sanctus from *Requiem for the Living*' from *The Complete Poems* by C. Day-Lewis (published by Sinclair-Stevenson); 'Going up the Line' by Martin Armstrong (published in *Buzzards* by Martin Secker, 1921); and 'Motorway' by Roger McGough.

Golgonooza Press for 'Childhood' by Kathleen Raine.

The Trustees of the Dunsany Will Trust for 'Snow on the East Wind' from *The Face of England* (published by Longmans) and 'A Call to the Wild' from *50 Poems* (published by G.P. Putnam) by Lord Dunsany.

Mr A.Beal, Literary Executor, for 'Leaving Town' and 'Beside the River' from *Collected Poems 1929-59* by James Reeves (published by Heinemann).

Anthony Thwaite for his poem 'The Foresters Arms' from *Inscriptions* (published by Oxford University Press).

Neil Astley for his poem 'Great North Road' (published by Morden Tower Publications, Throth).

Bernard Saint for his poem 'What I am' from *Children Of Albion* (published by Penguin).

Curtis Brown Group and the Estate of Vita Sackville-West for 'The Land — Winter' by Vita Sackville-West (first published 1927).

Harper Collins Publishers for 'A Talk with a Wood' from *Little Johnny's Confessions* and 'Frogs in the Wood' from *Grove Gossip* by Brian Patten (published by Allen & Unwin).

Bert Ward for his poem 'And send the time away' (published by London Voices Poetry Workshop in *The Rising Tide*).

Pan Macmillan for 'Fire' from *Collected Poems 1905-1925* by Wilfred Wilson Gibson.

C.S. Lewis Pte Ltd. for 'The Future of Forestry' by C.S. Lewis.

Spike Milligan Productions for 'Values '67' from *Small Dreams of a Scorpion* by Spike Milligan (published by Michael Joseph).

196

Allan Roddick and the Estate of Charles Brasch for 'The City' by Charles Brasch.

The Random House Group Ltd for 'The Line Gang' and 'Mowing' from *The Poetry of Robert Frost* (ed. Edward Connery Lathen, published by Jonathan Cape); 'Children by the River' from *The Slant Door* by George Szirtes; and 'The Coast: Norfolk' from *Collected Poems* by Frances Cornford (published by Cresset Press).

R. Geraint Gruffydd, Literary Executor, for 'Ascension Thursday' by Saunders Lewis; Gomer Press for the English translation by Gwyn Thomas, and for 'A Celebration' from *Ghost Country* by Herbert Williams.

Carcanet Press Ltd for 'Love Without Hope' and 'On Dwelling' from *Complete Poems* by Robert Graves; 'Forefathers' from *Selected Poems* by Edmund Blunden; 'The Shepherd's Hut' from *Selected Poems* by Andrew Young; 'Summer Song' from *Just like the Resurrection* by Patricia Beer (published by Macmillan); 'At Stoke' from *Selected Poems 1951–74* and 'Foxes' Moon' from *Under The Moon's Reign* by Charles Tomlinson (both published by Oxford University Press).

The Society of Authors acting on behalf of the estates of John Masefield, Laurence Binyon and Walter de la Mare for 'Midnight' from *Collected Poems* by John Masefield (published by Heinemann); 'The Burning of the Leaves' by Laurence Binyon; and 'All That's Past' from *Collected Poems* by Walter de la Mare (published by Faber).

David Higham for 'With People, So With Trees' from *Peake's Progress* by Mervyn Peake (published by Allen & Unwin); 'Oil' from *A Winter Visitor* by Pete Morgan (published by Secker & Warburg); and 'Fern Hill' from *Selected Poems* by Dylan Thomas (published by Dent & Sons).

George Sassoon for 'A View of Old Exeter', 'The Hawthorn Tree' and 'December Stillness' from *Collected Poems 1908-56* by Siegfried Sassoon.

DISCLAIMER

Every effort has been made to trace copyright holders of the poems published in this book, and especially the work of the poets listed below. The editor and publisher apologise if any material has been included without permission or without appropriate acknowledgement, and would be glad to be told of anyone who has not been consulted.

Peter Russell, 'Mnemosyne'

Edward Garfitt, 'Predators' (from *Drawn from the Wood*, 1987) and 'Magpies' (from *One for the Road*, 1987)

Heather Harrison, 'Green Man' (from *Beneath the Pavement*, 1987)

Margaret Buckle, 'The Old Thorn' and 'The Moorland Road' (from *Stonewall Country*, Yew Tree Press, 1980

Jesse Baggaley, 'The Restless People' (from *Rural Rhymes*, 1975)

Charles L Graves, 'Norfolk: A Study in Country Characteristics' (from *East Anglian Verse*, 1974)

Ann Taylor, 'Turnip Tops' (from *East Anglian Verse* 1974)

Bette McArdle, 'Rural School' (from *New Poetry Vol. 5*, Arts Council Anthologies)

R.N.Allan, 'Elegies' (from *New Poetry Vol. 1*, Arts Council Anthologies)

Jon Bye 'Taxonomy' (from *The Lore of Looking*, 1981)

Harold Massingham, 'Stickleback' (from *Black Bull Guarding Apples*, 1965)

Jinny Birkbeck, Editor of *The Listening Earth*
London, January 2003

THE SPONSORS OF THIS BOOK

This book has been made possible through the generosity of: Miss Sarah Anderson, The Arthur Stephens Charitable Trust, Mr Christopher Balfour, Mr James Barstow, The Simon Boyd Charitable Trust, Mrs Stanley Brodie, Burlington Slate Ltd, James Burnett of Leys, Mr Michael Boyle, Mr Andrew Buxton, Mr Gervase Buxton, Mr Charles Campbell, Valeria Viscountess Coke, Mr Rory Collins, Sir Richard Cory-Wright, the Hon. Mrs Roualeyn Cumming-Bruce, Mr & Mrs Anthony Darell-Brown, Mr Jason Emrich, The Family Assurance Company, Lord Charles Fitzroy, Mr Robin Fletcher, Colonel Paul Freeland, Mr Harry Garnett, Mr Robert Gladstone, Sir John Guinness, Mr Edward Harley, Mr Giles Harrap, Mr Sparrow Harrison, Mr Anthony Hudson, Mr Peter Kennedy, Mrs Judith Keppel, Messrs Knight Frank & Rutley, Mr John Lamb, Mr Anthony Leeming, Mr Robin Macinlay, Lord Maclay, Mrs Maltsby, Mrs Josephine Marston, Mr Christopher Masson, Mr Jamie McGrigor MSP, Mr Richard McKennell, The M.V. Millhouse Trust, Mr Robin Parish, Mr & Mrs Brian Peers, Lady Romayne Pike, Mrs Wout Rueb-Zernicker, Major Conway Seymour, Frances Lady Shelburne, The Countess of Snowdon, Mrs Michael Woodhouse.

The Rank Foundation Fund

The Rank Foundation Fund is administered by the ARC-Addington Fund which was initiated by the Archbishop of Canterbury in response to the financial problems facing the agricultural industry in 2001 as a result of the foot and mouth epidemic. It was very clear from the early stages of the outbreak that, with the countryside virtually closed down, other industries were just as badly affected, yet there was very little or no financial support available. The Rank Foundation made a very generous donation to enable help to be provided for this sector in the form of the Rank Foundation Fund.

The occupations of applicants have been many and varied. Amongst these diverse trades have been eel fishing, plastic film recycling, carriage building and taxidermy, in addition to the more obviously hard hit industries such as tourism and leisure. The effect of foot and mouth on the rural economy was aptly demonstrated by one Devon accountant who said that, although he had no farmers on his books, fifty per cent of his clients had been affected by the consequences. The grants allocated have been used for various purposes. Many applicants have simply needed money to cover day to day living expenses. Others have been particularly concerned with keeping their business in the public eye and have needed additional advertising. In some instances we have been asked to make out the cheque to a person other than the beneficiary, such as a landlord who was owed rent or an apprentice who has had to accept severely reduced wages. We feel in these cases our help has had a "knock-on" effect, going some way to counteract the far-reaching consequences of foot and mouth.

The Rank Foundation Fund grants are now directed towards training or capital expenditure in new ventures. An example of this is in a village where neither the shop nor the pub is viable, but by combining the two and incorporating the Post Office a thriving business is possible, to the benefit of the entire community.

As the immediate effects of foot and mouth recede, it has become apparent that there is an underlying, long-term problem in the countryside which the ARC-Addington Fund, together with the Rank Foundation Fund, hopes to address. It has become apparent from the information on the application forms that many rural businesses are carrying an unsustainable level of debt and are simply not viable. The failure of these would frequently entail the loss of the family home. Often the only available local authority housing, if indeed there is any, is in an inappropriate setting for those accustomed to a rural existence. The intention is to identify individuals who require help and then to provide housing where it is needed and thus keep people within their locality. This will enable people to exit their business with some degree of dignity and will contribute to the continuation of a thriving rural community.

The Rank Foundation Fund can be contacted at:
The ARC-Addington Fund, Stoneleigh Park, Warwickshire CV8 2LZ

A LITTLE PIECE OF ENGLAND
John Jackson

A wonderful account of the many trials and tribulations of running your own smallholding, by the Chairman of The Countryside Alliance. Over £7 from each book sold goes to the Countryside Alliance.

Hardback **£12.95**

THE TOWNIES' GUIDE TO THE COUNTRYSIDE
Jill Mason

Packed with facts and information about all aspects of rural Britain, presented in a clear and helpful way. Written by one of the country's few women gamekeepers. Publication Sept 2003.   Hardback **£20**

THE POACHER'S COOKBOOK
Prue Coats (with illustrations by Barbara Greg)

A companion volume to *The Poacher's Handbook*, this collection of game and country recipes has become a cookery classic in its own right.   Paperback **£11.99**

AUTUMN ROAD TO THE ISLES
'BB'

In 1958 BB set out with his wife in their ancient landrover and caravan for an autumn journey to the remote highlands of Scotland. More than a travel book, more than a nature book, *Autumn Road to the Isles* remains a classic since its original issue in 1959.

Hardback **£14.95**

THE WAY OF A COUNTRYMAN
Ian Niall (with illustrations by CF Tunnicliffe)

Ian Niall conveys with graphic insight the joy of the countryside in these memories of a lifetime's shooting and fishing. A collection of essays on country matters with many charming and amusing anecdotes.   Hardback **£15.95**

THE WHITE ROAD WESTWARDS
'BB'

Over 40 years ago BB set off with his landrover to wander through the lanes and byways of Western England. Whether listening to nightingales in Savernake Forest or watching badgers on the high cliffs of Gurnard's Head in Cornwall, he captures the scents and country scenes around him, each day filled with new delight.   Hardback **£14.95**

REFLECTIONS OF A COUNTRYMAN
Fred J Taylor

Fred J Taylor, the genuine original countryman, shares recollections of his country childhood, travel and outdoor adventures. This evergreen, now in its fourth printing, still has a wide following.
                                                        Hardback **£16.95**

All these books are available by direct mail from
Merlin Unwin Books, 7 Corve Street, Ludlow,
Shropshire SY8 1DB, UK
Tel: 01584 877456
Fax: 01584 877457
For a complete list of country books see our
website: www.countrybooksdirect.com